'THE TEARS OF ORPHANS'

No future without human rights

AI Index: AFR 54/02/95

ISBN: 0 86210 238 3

First published in January 1995 by
Amnesty International Publications
1 Easton Street
London WC1X 8DJ
United Kingdom

Copyright:
    Amnesty International 1995
    Publications

Original language: English

All rights reserved

No part of this publication
may be reproduced, stored
in a retrieval system, or
transmitted in any form or by
any means electronic,
mechanical, photo-
copying, recording and/or
otherwise, without the prior
permission of the publishers.

Printed by: Flashprint Enterprises Ltd.

CONTENTS

GLOSSARY v

INTRODUCTION 1

1 CRUSHING OPPOSITION 9
The security apparatus 10
Patterns of repression 12
The dismantling of civil society 15
Political parties 15
Trade unions 18
Students 19
The judiciary 20
Lawyers 21
Controlling the press 22

2 THE APPARATUS OF REPRESSION 25
A legal veneer 25
Torture and ill-treatment 26
Deaths in detention 30
Sexual abuse 31
Torture as policy 31
Unfair trials 32
Unfair trials in military courts 33
Unfair trials in civilian courts 35

3 'NATIONAL SALVATION' 39
Dealing with the displaced 40
Rounding up street children 41
Cruel, inhuman or degrading punishments 42
Flogging 43
Amputation and other forms of mutilation 46
The death penalty 49

4 THE DESTRUCTION OF THE SOUTH 53
The roots of conflict 55
The place of religion in the war 56
Human rights violations in the war zones 57
The creation of humanitarian need 62
Killings and 'disappearances' in Juba 64
'Disappearances' in Khartoum 66
The treatment of captured SPLA soldiers 67
Torture in southern Sudan 67

5 EXPLOITING ETHNICITY 71
The hidden war in northern Bahr al-Ghazal 71
The fate of women and children abducted
in northern Bahr al-Ghazal 76
Laying waste to the Nuba mountains 78
The *jihad* against the Nuba 79
Destroying Nuba leadership 83

6 'THE NEW SUDAN': HUMAN RIGHTS ABUSES BY THE SPLA 87
SPLA abuses in the Nuba mountains 87
The split in the SPLA 89
Killings by both factions in Upper Nile 89
Killings of civilians by SPLA-Mainstream
in Eastern Equatoria 94
Human rights abuses after the split 95
The arrest of suspected dissidents 97
Action against human rights abusers 99
The administration of justice by the SPLA 99

7 RESPONDING TO HUMAN RIGHTS CRITICISM 105
International human rights mechanisms
and Sudan 108
A strategic response 111
Human rights and peace 115
A proposal for action 117

8 CONCLUSIONS AND RECOMMENDATIONS 121
I. Recommendations to the government and
both factions of the SPLA 122
II. Recommendations to the international
community 128

ENDNOTES 130

APPENDIX
Sudan's obligations under international law 131

GLOSSARY

DUP —Democratic Unionist Party
FSWTU —Federation of Sudanese Workers' Trades Unions
FSEP —Federation of Sudanese Employees and Professionals
ICRC —International Committee of the Red Cross
ICCPR —International Covenant on Civil and Political Rights
IGADD —Inter-governmental Authority on Drought and Development
ILO —International Labour Organisation
IMF —International Monetary Fund
NDA —National Democratic Alliance
NIF —National Islamic Front
NSA —National Security Act
OAU —Organization of African Unity
OLF —Oromo Liberation Front [Ethiopia]
OLS —Operation Lifeline Sudan
PDF —Popular Defence Force
SCP —Sudan Communist Party
SNP —Sudan National Party
SPLA —Sudan People's Liberation Army[1]
TNA —Transitional National Assembly
UN —United Nations
WFP —World Food Program

---

[1] In September 1994 SPLA-United, led by Dr Riek Machar Teny-Dhurgon, changed its name to the South Sudan Independence Army (SSIA).

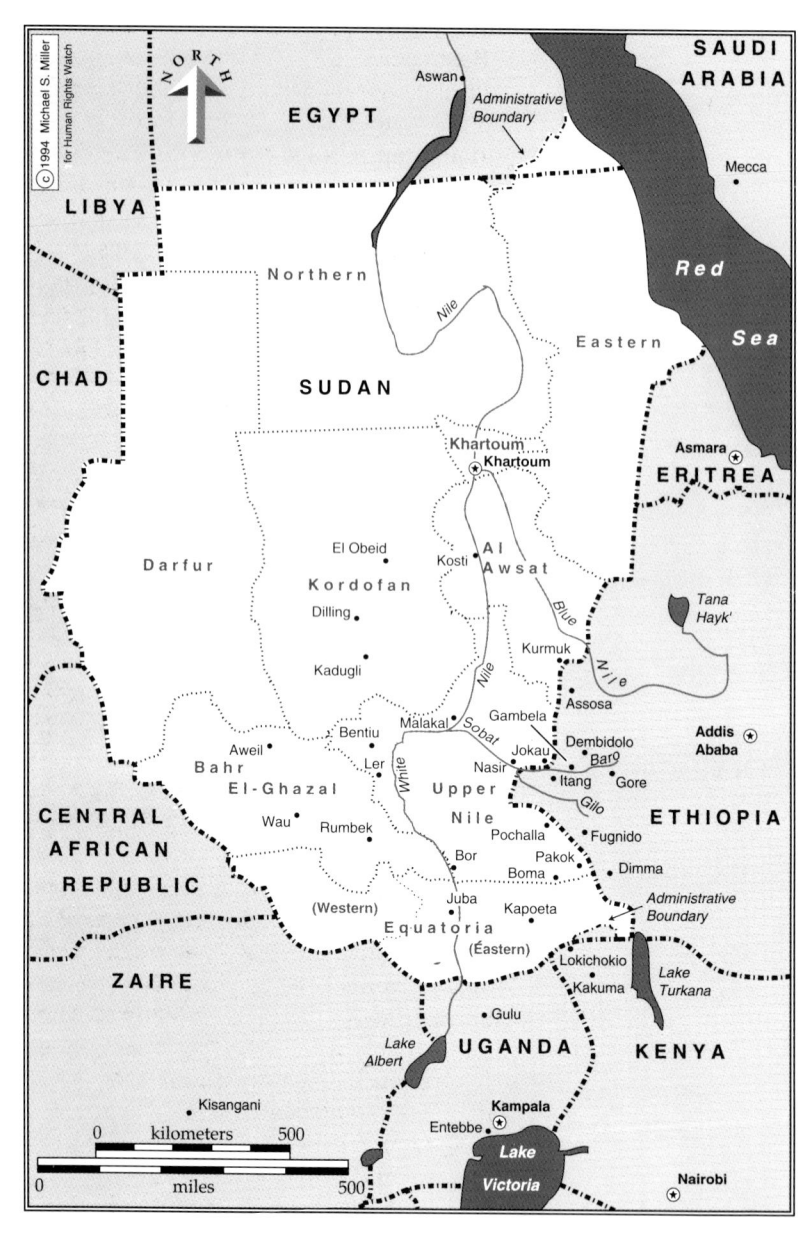

Sudan

INTRODUCTION

Before dawn on 30 June 1989 Sudan army units led by Brigadier Omar Hassan Ahmad al-Bashir closed the airport, seized the presidential palace and the army headquarters, and set up road-blocks throughout Khartoum, Sudan's capital city. Within hours rebel units had arrested a score of leading politicians. A state of emergency was declared, the Constitution suspended and political parties and trade unions dissolved. The independent press was closed down and all secular associ-ations were suspended. The new leaders announced the formation of the National Salvation Revolution Command Council to govern the country.

So ended three years of multi-party democracy in Sudan. Those three years were deeply problematic for human rights, with the country sharply divided. Political freedoms were largely respected in the north, but human rights were grossly abused in southern Sudan and other areas where the government and the armed opposition movement, the Sudan People's Liberation Army (SPLA), were locked in a fierce internal war. However, the coming to power of the military government ushered in a new era of human rights violations characterized by a range and scale of abuse unprecedented in Sudan's history.

Since 30 June 1989 virtually all sectors of Sudanese society in all parts of the country have experienced the persistent and gross violation of human rights. Virtually every kind of human rights violation of concern to Amnesty International has been perpetrated by a political and security establishment that behaves as if it is unaccountable. Most of these violations are taking place outside the framework of both Sudanese and international law.

The country remains deeply divided. The war continues in the south and adjacent areas such as the Nuba mountains. The SPLA is split

'THE TEARS OF ORPHANS'

Sudan's military leader Lieutenant-General Omar Hassan Ahmad al-Bashir. © *Associated Press*

into two factions which are at war with each other as well as the government. Political opposition has been forced underground in Khartoum and other major cities in northern Sudan.

The government has also embarked upon an ambitious program to reshape Sudanese society, particularly in the north, according to a political agenda derived from its interpretation of Islam. It has resorted to repression to maintain control. Hundreds of prisoners of conscience from all walks of life have been arrested and detained without charge or trial. Torture and degrading treatment in secret detention centres, known locally as "ghost houses", have been widespread and sometimes fatal. Political prisoners charged and brought to court have been tried unfairly before military tribunals and, more recently, in civilian courts staffed by a subverted and compliant judiciary. Prisoners convicted of both criminal and political crimes at unfair summary military trials have been executed since 1989. Suspected political opponents have been sacked from their jobs and lost their homes, had their property confiscated and their civil rights restricted. In 1991 the government introduced a penal

INTRODUCTION

code which provides for cruel, inhuman and degrading penalties: flogging, amputation and stoning to death. Thousands of floggings, many of them of women, have taken place since the government seized power.

The current war between primarily southern-based rebels and the northern-based government began in 1983, but there have been only 11 years of peace since 1956.

The war has been prosecuted with rigour and ruthlessness on both sides. The security forces have deliberately attacked civilians, killing them, driving them from their land, looting and destroying their means of livelihood. Thousands of people have been extrajudicially executed or have "disappeared". In the Nuba mountains, a remote region in the heart of the country, the government has systematically implemented a strategy of forcible relocation of whole communities to so-called "peace villages" controlled by the army and the government-created Popular Defence Force (PDF) militia. Women and children have been abducted and sold into domestic slavery by government-controlled militia. In towns under government control in the conflict zones, there has been little respect for the due process of

SPLA-United is led by Dr Riek Machar Teny-Dhurgon. © *Peter Moszynski*

Dr John Garang de Mabior is the leader of SPLA-Mainstream. © *Panos*

3

'THE TEARS OF ORPHANS'

law; people suspected of opposing the government have been detained, "disappeared" and extrajudicially executed.

This is a war which takes few prisoners. It appears that both the government and SPLA routinely and deliberately kill people captured in combat.

Both factions of the SPLA, SPLA-Mainstream and SPLA-United, have deliberately attacked and killed civilians, creating a cycle of violence and revenge by pitting community against community. Both appear to lack command systems capable of maintaining control of their military. Both have internal systems which are applied arbitrarily according to the whim of local commanders. The SPLA-Mainstream leadership has been ruthless in its drive to acquire and maintain its position. Prominent dissidents within its ranks have been detained and in some cases executed. Prisoners held by the SPLA have been tortured, sometimes to death. Both groups have summarily executed soldiers or individuals suspected of supporting the rival faction. There are persistent reports that prisoners captured on the battlefield have been subsequently murdered.

The war has created a catastrophe of immense human cost as all parties flagrantly violate human rights and the humanitarian laws and principles governing armed conflict. Deliberate assaults on civilians by government forces and both factions of the SPLA have created a humanitarian disaster in the conflict zones. In 1994 the United Nations (UN), which runs a major humanitarian relief operation called Operation Lifeline Sudan (OLS), estimated that more than two million war-affected people would need food aid during the year and more than five million would need non-food aid. The violation of human rights lies at the heart of the creation of humanitarian need.

The military government has sought to deflect human rights criticism by accusing its critics of being motivated by a desire to oppose or insult Islam. This message exploits the beliefs and values of the Muslim majority in Sudan, and Muslims in other countries, as the government tries to deflect criticism and to build public support. The Special Rapporteur appointed by the UN Commissioner for Human Rights in March 1993 to investigate the human rights situation in Sudan has been described by the government as an "anti-Muslim fanatic".

Amnesty International takes no position on the political goals or ideology of either the government or opposition. The organization

INTRODUCTION

Dinka fishermen at Apeth, Bahr al-Ghazal, in southern Sudan.
© *David Stewart-Smith/Katz*

works on behalf of the human rights of all people in Sudan, whether they be Muslims or Christians, opponents of the government or its supporters. Its concerns arise when those in authority violate internationally recognized human rights standards.

Sudan is one of the world's poorest countries. Two thirds of its 26 million people are Muslims but the country contains extraordinary religious and ethnic diversity. Some 400 languages are spoken, although Arabic is the popular common language in both north and south and the first language of many northerners. Most northerners are Muslims and many claim Arab origins. Others, however, such as the Nuba of South Kordofan, the Fur of Darfur and the people of Blue Nile province, identify themselves as non-Arab Africans. The south, which comprises the states of Bahr al-Ghazal, Upper Nile and Equatoria, is even more religiously and ethnically diverse than the north; the Dinka and the Nuer form the majority but there are many other smaller ethnic groups. Most educated southerners espouse Christianity, although some are Muslim. Most of the rural population follow their own religious traditions.

The labels Arab and African, Muslim and Christian, even northerner and southerner, have become intensely politicized during the struggle to forge a national identity. Ethnic and religious identities are important factors in the deep political cleavages running through Sudanese society. They are used to mobilize political support, to assert difference, to claim superiority, to determine access to power and to define enemies. Both factions of the SPLA have become increasingly dominated by leaderships of particular ethnic origins.

A consistent pattern of human rights abuse in Sudan is clear, although verifying some individual reports in a country so vast, so poor and so deeply divided can be difficult. People from virtually every walk of life in Sudan are at risk of human rights abuse by those in authority, whether in the war zones, in areas controlled by the government, in areas controlled by the armed opposition or in areas far from the war and little affected by it. Each instance of abuse exacerbates political divisions and breeds hatred. The future of Sudan depends upon establishing respect for human rights. Without that respect there can be little hope of success in establishing the mutual trust required to solve Sudan's many political problems.

*Within my chest is a lying radio: this is my homeland
Offering miserable people
Water from a fleeing illusion.
By the Nile lives our dark city;
It has turned it into
A bog of flies and sewers.
Having seen me, the hospital said
to its porter: Take him
to the healing hospital of Azrael, the angel of death,
This is an order;
Go and testify, willingly or through torture, if you wish,
against your rebellious soul.
Your denial is of no use.
In your grave enjoy
oblivion.*

Mohamed al-Mahdi Majzoub, from the poem *Defeat ... Victory.*
Reproduced with permission of *Afaq Jadeeda* magazine

1

Crushing opposition

"I vow here before you to purge from our ranks the renegades, the hirelings, enemies of the people and enemies of the armed forces...Anyone who betrays this nation does not deserve the honour of living."

Omar Hassan Ahmad al-Bashir, Sudan's Head of State, at a public rally in December 1989

Civil society is under attack in Sudan as the military government consolidates its control and seeks to reshape social institutions according to its ideological program of radical Islam. Part of this process is the crushing of political opposition. Thousands of Sudanese citizens have spent periods in detention since June 1989. Many have been tortured.

The government has promised that general elections will be held in March 1995, after which martial law will be lifted. In the meantime, emergency legislation prohibits "any political opposition by any means to the regime of the Revolution for National Salvation". The legislation bans strikes and unauthorized political meetings. It allows the authorities to arrest anyone or restrict his or her movements without warrant. Detention without charge or trial is also provided for under the 1990 National Security Act.

Anyone suspected of opposition to the government or its policies is at risk of arrest. This is as true in the major cities and rural areas of northern Sudan as it is in the war zones. Displaced southerners, refugees, members of Muslim religious orders that do not conform to the government's interpretation of Islam, lawyers, members of the military, women protesting at the cost of living, students protesting at changes in their allowances, trade unionists, political activists, journalists, foreign nationals, musicians, artists, and many others have been detained.

'THE TEARS OF ORPHANS'

A camel herder in northern Sudan. © *Peter Charlesworth/Panos*

Some have subsequently been convicted of political offences at unfair trials; the majority have simply been held without charge for weeks, months and sometimes years.

The security apparatus

One of the new government's first priorities was to ensure control of the military and security forces. After the coup, the High Command and hundreds of other army officers were dismissed. The paramilitary PDF was created to provide a parallel military force of ideological supporters of the government. A parallel security force, the Security of the Revolution, was also formed. This shadowy organization, staffed by young supporters of the National Islamic Front (NIF), the radical Islamic party that provides the government with its ideological inspiration, took the lead in the mass arrest of suspected government opponents while the official Sudan Security Service was purged. The shadowy groups that headed the consolidation of the new government appear now to have been merged with the formal security bodies while retaining links with key officials through presidential advisers on security.

Political opponents are held without charge or trial in civil prisons run by the Sudan Prisons Service, in unofficial secret detention centres run by the security services — known as "ghost houses" — and in regular security offices such as the security headquarters in Khartoum. Former prisoners held in civil prisons

CHAPTER 1

Women in the Popular Defence Force militia training at Khartoum airport.
© *Abbas/Magnum*

Sudanese soldiers and civilians stand in front of Kober Prison in Khartoum. Hundreds of political prisoners have been held in Kober Prison since the government seized power on 30 June 1989. © *Popperfoto*

'THE TEARS OF ORPHANS'

report that, despite the sometimes harsh conditions in jails, physical ill-treatment by prison guards is not common. The detention centres and offices of the security services, where the vast majority of suspected political opponents are held, are an entirely different matter.

Year after year, detainees report experiencing or witnessing torture in "ghost houses" and security offices. Some have died as a result. The authorities claim they take a firm stand against torture and ill-treatment, but the reported pattern of beatings, burnings, harsh physical exercises and grotesque forms of humiliation remains consistent.

Government claims that detainees are not held in security centres are flatly contradicted by the testimony of former detainees. Many do not know exactly where they were held — neither detainees nor their families are told where they are or which authority is holding them — but they do know that they were not being held in civil prisons. An array of government-owned and sometimes private buildings have been used as detention centres. Some of these have become formal detention centres; others appear to be used when the number of detainees requires it.

The conditions of detention reported by many former detainees amount to cruel, inhuman or degrading treatment, prohibited by international standards. Many report being held in grossly overcrowded conditions. Others describe being held in solitary confinement, sometimes in latrines or small closets. A detainee held for four months in mid-1992 described his experience in a letter written after his release:

> "Have you ever tried to shut yourself in a toilet for four months...The temperature can reach $100°F$ [$40°C$] And added to that there is the foul smell of your own body. And the fatal loneliness, and sadness, sadness. And the fatal feeling of being defeated. The silence in a room (ha! ha!) not more than 1m by 1.5m. Exactly the size of a prayer mat. I was enjoying the periods of torture because I could smell fresh air, because the place of being beaten was outside. Most of the time."

Patterns of repression

Some political prisoners have spent more than two years in jail but most have been held for periods lasting between a few weeks and

CHAPTER 1

several months. Many suspected government opponents have been detained on several separate occasions, sometimes being rearrested only days after being released. Others have experienced a system of physical restriction which consists of making suspected dissidents report daily, early in the morning, to the security services. They are then made to wait until the evening, normally without being questioned or provided with food or water. This form of restriction on an individual's freedom of movement can last from a few weeks to several months.

The pattern of arrest and release, the use of secret detention centres and the poor communications that exist between different parts of Sudan make it difficult to establish exactly how many political prisoners are in detention at any particular time. The information that reaches the outside world tends to be about political activists from the capital or other major cities. Since 1989 Amnesty International has learned the names of some 1,500 political detainees held at different times, mainly in Khartoum. Some of them were prisoners of conscience. These represent only part of the total number of people arrested around the country.

Hundreds of political prisoners were arrested in 1989 and 1990. In late March 1990 at least 35 leading members of the Umma Party — the political wing of the *Ansar* Islamic order — and senior members of the armed forces discharged after the coup were among those arrested on suspicion of conspiring to overthrow the government. In May 23 army officers were imprisoned after summary trials in military courts. Also in May, railway workers went on strike in Atbara and several trade unionists were arrested. In November hundreds were arrested for their participation in anti-government demonstrations and strikes in several northern cities.

Although the authorities released 299 detainees in May and June 1991, the pattern of arrests continued. At least six detainees, members of the Sudan Communist Party (SCP) and the Sudan National Party (SNP) which draws its support from the Nuba of South Kordofan, were rearrested within days. By the end of the year Amnesty International had identified more than 200 people detained since May. The names of many more political prisoners remained unknown to the organization. Dozens — students, trade unionists, journalists, musicians, artists — were arrested after demonstrations in July at Khartoum University. In September trade unionists were arrested after further disturbances at Khartoum

'THE TEARS OF ORPHANS'

Khartoum, the capital of Sudan, is located at the confluence of the Blue and White Niles. ©Betty Press/Panos

University. Other trade unionists were arrested in November on suspicion of distributing anti-government leaflets.

Amnesty International recorded the names of more than 250 political prisoners detained during 1992 in Khartoum alone. Umma Party members arrested in January were held until September. In April women relatives of army officers executed in 1990 for allegedly planning a coup were held for up to three weeks after they staged a demonstration. In May journalists, lawyers, artists and a television producer were arrested. In June at least 37 detainees, including Egyptians, an Algerian and a Palestinian, were being held in a "ghost house" in Khartoum. In December women demonstrating in Omdurman against the effects of the poor economic situation were briefly detained. At least four were then made to report daily to the security offices. In the same month SCP members were detained; nine were not released until March 1994, two others remained in detention as of October 1994.

In 1993 journalists were arrested in January and March. Between April and June scores of people were detained in northern towns in what appears to have been a concerted attack on members of the *Ansar* Islamic order and its political expression, the Umma Party. In August more members of the Umma Party were arrested.

In November women seeking to present a petition to the UN Special Rapporteur on Sudan as he visited Khartoum were arrested in front of him. Two were dragged along the ground before being bundled into police vans. They were later released.

The pattern of arrest and short-term detention of political prisoners continued during 1994. By the end of September Amnesty International had confirmed more than 100 arrests in Khartoum. Activists from the SCP and the Umma Party, journalists, trade unionists, lawyers and others staging anti-government demonstrations were detained for periods ranging from a few weeks to several months. Four aid workers, Egyptian Christians working with displaced people in squatter camps around Khartoum, were arrested in April. They were released after three weeks, but three were expelled from Sudan. At least 22 serving and retired army officers were arrested in June and July and reportedly accused of plotting a coup. All were held in incommunicado detention.

The dismantling of civil society

The continuing pattern of arrests is taking place in the context of a reshaping of civil society according to the will of the military and their radical Islamic supporters. The civil service, trade unions, the judiciary, educational institutions and the media have all been purged. Institutional structures have been created which ensure that political supporters of the government have overwhelming influence.

Political parties

Sudan has a long tradition of party political activism and members and supporters of political parties have been particular targets for the security services, as the authorities have sought to crush organized opposition.

At the time of the 1989 coup, two political parties based on Islam and led by family dynasties had long dominated Sudanese political life. They are the Umma Party, led by Sadiq al-Mahdi, who had been Prime Minister at the time of the coup, and the Democratic Unionist Party (DUP), led by Mohamed Osman al-Mirghani. Although numerically much smaller, the SCP is also politically influential because of a well-organized trade union membership. There are many smaller secular parties. These include a variety of left-

'THE TEARS OF ORPHANS'

wing groupings, for example the Ba'th Arab Socialist Party, several southern Sudanese-based parties and the SNP.

All parties were banned when the military took power in 1989 and trade unions were suspended. The government has since indicated that elections will be held in March 1995, but that Sudan will not return to a multi-party political system. The assets and property of political parties remain confiscated.

Despite the ban, the major political parties remain politically active underground. In October 1989 political parties and trade unions set up the National Democratic Alliance (NDA) to provide an umbrella for opposition to the new government.

Hundreds of party activists and trade unionists have been detained without charge, released and redetained. Each month there are new arrests. In the first six months of 1994, scores of opposition party activists were arrested and held uncharged in Khartoum alone. Some were held for 24 hours; others spent several months in detention.

Sadiq al-Mahdi, the Umma Party's leader, was held for 24 hours in April 1994 and then for 13 days in June and July. Other Umma Party members were arrested in February. At least two, al-Fadil Adam Ismail, secretary general of the youth wing, and Abdallah Barakat, an imam in the *Ansar* Islamic order, had been arrested several times before. In April Sarah Nugdallah, a member of the Umma Party's women's and executive committees, was detained for 10 weeks. Also in April Abdel Rasoul al-Nur, the former governor of Kordofan province who had spent long periods in detention in previous years, was detained and released after a few days and then rearrested in late May. He was released in late June after falling ill. More Umma Party members were arrested in late May.

Members of other political parties were arrested during the first half of 1994. In February Osman Omar al-Sharif, former Minister of Justice and prominent DUP member, was transferred to a "ghost house" in Khartoum after he had been held for 11 days at security offices in Wad Medani, Sudan's second city. It is believed he was released in April. He had previously spent two years in prison between 1989 and 1991 after being convicted of corruption at an unfair military trial. In late 1993 he was detained for a month on suspicion of instigating a strike by merchants in Wad Medani.

Activists from the SCP have been regular targets for the security services. Since 1989 dozens have been arrested, detained for several months and released. Party members arrested in 1994 include

CHAPTER 1

Farouq Mosque, Khartoum. The majority of people living in northern Sudan are Muslims. © *Hutchison*

'THE TEARS OF ORPHANS'

Mahjoub Mohamed Sharif, popularly known as "the people's poet", Bushra 'Abd al-Karim, the secretary general of the Sudanese Youth Union, and Salah al-A'alim, a trade unionist. Mahjoub Mohamed Sharif was reportedly released in August 1994. SCP members Farouq Ali Zacharia and Salah Hassan Samerait, arrested in December 1992, remained in detention without charge or trial in October 1994, as did Yousif Hussein, arrested in June 1993.

Trade unions

Scores of trade unionists have been arrested, questioned, held uncharged, released and then rearrested each year since 1989. Dr Magdi Mohamedani, active in the suspended Doctors' Union, was detained between February and April 1994. He had also been arrested in August 1992 and late 1989. In March 1994 Kamal Abdelwahab Nur al-Dayem, an activist in the banned Teachers' Union, was picked up and held until May. In late 1993 he had been made to report daily to a security office in Khartoum North. In June 1994 Ali al-Mahi al-Sakhi, president of the Central Mint Workers' Union, was among six activists arrested in Khartoum. This was at least his third period of detention. In August trade unionists active in the Sudan Telecommunications Corporation were detained after a strike.

Many trade unionists have been arrested during the government's attempt to establish trade union structures which are under its control. Before the army seized power trade unions were organized in most sectors of employment. The two largest trade union federations, the Federation of Sudanese Workers' Trades Unions (FSWTU) and the Federation of Sudanese Employees and Professionals (FSEP) claimed a combined membership of three million people. In September 1989 the new government announced its intention to reorganize Sudan's trade unions.

A Trade Unions Dialogue Conference of government-appointed delegates was convened in August 1990. The conference declared its support for the government and announced that strikes were "a weapon of destruction and sabotage". In February 1992 these recommendations became the Workers' Trades Union Act which established a trade union regulator, appointed by the Head of State, with extensive powers to intervene in internal union affairs. The regulator is responsible for authorizing the creation, and the closure, of trade unions and cancelling their elections should the authorities deem it necessary. In September 1992 supervisory committees were set up and in October elections were held.

A campaign of intimidation and arrest during trade union elections in October 1992 ensured that the only candidates to stand in the elections were known government supporters. Over 50 trade unionists were detained for protesting against election procedures. Prominent trade union activists who were held in "ghost houses" included Dr Mokhtar Fadul, brother of Dr Ali Fadul who was tortured to death in April 1990. Other union members were made to report daily to security offices during the election period. At least 21 were made to report each day until December 1992.

Students

There have been regular disturbances at the universities since 30 June 1989 with demonstrations against government policy, dismissals of academic staff and poor conditions, leading to arrests and expulsions. In December 1989 the security services opened fire on a demonstration by students from Khartoum University, killing two.

In late November 1990 Gezira University students staged a strike and protest marches in Wad Medani after the government-appointed Vice-Chancellor had dismissed eight lecturers and suspended free board and lodging for students. On their first march, the students held a sit-down protest outside Wad Medani hospital. About 100 were arrested. The women were released within hours but 66 men were taken to al-Farouq, a PDF training camp, where each received 30 lashes before being released.

During a day of action in the town on 28 November, 34 students were arrested. Seventeen men and an equal number of women students were taken to al-Farouq. There each was given 30 lashes on the orders of the deputy governor of Wad Medani. The women were further humiliated by being flogged in front of their male colleagues. After each man was flogged his head was partly shaved. At least two women required hospital treatment. Hundreds of other students were arrested on campus and detained for up to six days.

In July 1991 serious unrest erupted at Khartoum University over changes in the provision of board and lodging. The security services again suppressed the demonstrations with force; two students were killed and at least 40 students were detained. Some 13 student leaders were expelled.

In September 1991 the Khartoum University Students' Union

'THE TEARS OF ORPHANS'

was banned. In February 1992 students protested against the ban by refusing to sit examinations. In the following weeks at least 30 students were arrested. By May around 300 students had reportedly been expelled.

In late 1993 the ban on the students' union was lifted. Elections were held in November for executive positions, which were won by supporters of the government amid allegations of extensive ballot-rigging. Three days of student demonstrations culminated in clashes with the police and more than 350 arrests. Most were released within hours but at least 33 were taken to the security headquarters where they were beaten. Some were held without charge for more than six weeks.

The judiciary

Until 30 June 1989 the independence of Sudan's judiciary was firmly established in the Constitution. Since the coup the independence of the judiciary has been undermined through constitutional changes, purges and the creation of a system of parallel courts controlled by the military authorities.

Immediately after the coup the political authorities assumed wide-ranging powers over the appointment of judges, including the appointment of the Chief Justice and members of the Higher Judicial Council, the previously independent body of judges responsible for the regulation of the judiciary. Several judges suspected of opposing the new government's policies were dismissed. In August 1989 the judiciary went on strike and submitted a memorandum to the government demanding the dissolution of the military courts and seeking guarantees of non-interference by the authorities in judicial affairs. By then 58 judges had been dismissed from all levels of the judiciary. More than 100 judges resigned in protest at the dismissals. The protests were ignored and another 200 judges have since been purged. They have been replaced by political appointees, thus ensuring a compliant judiciary.

Between 1989 and 1991 a variety of special courts were created to try offences under the emergency regulations. Military courts set up in July 1989 to try civilians were presided over by three army officers and did not allow defence representation. In September these were replaced by Revolutionary Security Courts. In December 1989 new special courts were created, initially in Khartoum but by mid-1990 in other parts of the country. The authorities claimed these courts allowed defence representation and appeal. In reality,

CHAPTER 1

defence lawyers were allowed to be present in the court-room and to speak to their clients but were not allowed to address the court. Hearings frequently lasted only a few minutes. Appeals were to the Chief Justice and not to a higher court. Procedures in all these courts were summary and unfair. They were used to try both political and criminal cases.

In July 1991 the authorities announced that these special courts had been abolished. However, this did not end summary trials in Sudan. Soldiers and civilians accused of plotting a coup in August 1991 were summarily tried by courts-martial in October 1991. The authorities claim that some of more than 300 military personnel and civilians arrested in Juba in mid-1992 after SPLA incursions into the city were tried by courts-martial. Prisoners sentenced in courts-martial describe summary hearings lasting only a few minutes before military personnel unversed in the law, without any right to appeal, or to defence; in effect, these are not trials at all, but sentencing sessions.

Public Order Courts, a category of special court created in January 1990 by the Chief Justice, have not been abolished and are responsible for hearing cases involving breaches of national laws and local by-laws governing petty offences. They can impose fines and sentences of flogging and imprisonment. The courts sit in continuous session and sentences are handed down summarily and immediately.

Lawyers

The assault on lawyers has been as decisive as the attack on the judiciary. Like other professional associations and trade unions, the Sudan Bar Association, which had a long history of independence and human rights activism, was suspended on 30 June 1989 and replaced with a steering committee. The Bar Association premises were briefly used as a detention centre. In January 1993 the authorities announced that the Bar Association was to become a general union of Sudanese lawyers subject to the same controls as other government-created trade unions. Elections, boycotted by supporters of the suspended Bar Association, were held in March 1993.

Lawyers were among the first people detained after the coup. Scores more have been detained over succeeding years and some have been tortured. Those arrested in 1994 include Ali Mahmud Hassanein, a prominent lawyer who took a leading role in the defence of 12 men tried in early 1994 on charges of conspiring to cause acts of sabotage. He was detained for two weeks, apparently in an attempt to intimidate him from taking a role in political trials. Yousif Attiya was arrested in Khartoum in July 1994 and held for several weeks without charge or trial.

Controlling the press

During 1988, 20 daily newspapers, 15 weeklies and several monthly magazines were published in Sudan in Arabic and English. Immediately after the coup, all newspapers except the armed forces publication *al-Quwat al-Musallan* (Armed Forces) were closed down and several journalists were detained.

In August 1989 two daily newspapers produced by the Ministry of Culture and Information, *al-Inqaz al-Watani* (National Salvation) and *Sudan al-Hadith* (Modern Sudan), commenced publication and the authorities indicated that sports, trade and cultural publications were to be allowed. In October the official English-language monthly current affairs magazine, *Sudanow*, recommenced publication.

Scores of journalists and print-workers have spent periods in detention, in some cases for continuing the clandestine production of banned newspapers. In May 1992 journalists suspected of producing underground copies of *al-Hedaf* (The Target), the newspaper of the Ba'th Arab Socialist Party, were detained and held for periods ranging from several months to nearly two years, in apparent contravention of the government's own regulations on detention. One journalist, Ali Ahmad Hamdan, was held until April 1994.

In both March 1992 and April 1993 the authorities announced that independent newspapers would be allowed in Sudan once the appropriate legislation for their licensing had been approved. Later in 1993 a Press and Publications Act was passed which allows the publication of newspapers licensed by the National Council for Press and Publications. The council, appointed by the Head of State, is charged with ensuring that "sectarian" or "partisan" entities (in other words, political parties that are likely to oppose the government) do not publish in Sudan. As with all legislation in Sudan, the Press and Publications Act is secondary to the provisions of the emergency regulations.

In January 1994 Sudan's first independent newspaper, *al-Sudani al-Dawliyya* (Sudanese International), started publication.

CHAPTER 1

The experiment was short-lived. Although in broad ideological agreement with the government, *al-Sudani al-Dawliyya* did not shrink from criticizing specific government policies. The news editor was arrested in February 1994 and detained until 19 April. In early April the authorities invoked the emergency regulations and banned the newspaper. Three journalists were detained until June, including Mahjoub Mohamed al-Hassan Erwa, the newspaper's owner and editor, who was also stripped of membership of the Transitional National Assembly (TNA), Sudan's government-appointed interim parliament.

On 23 June 1994 Mohamed Abdulsid, a journalist with *al-Khartoum* newspaper which is published in Cairo, was arrested in Khartoum shortly after he had interviewed Umma Party leader Sadiq al-Mahdi. Mohamed Abdulsid was reportedly kicked and beaten in his office before being taken away. In September 1994 the government closed *al-Khartoum's* office in Khartoum. Mohamed Abdulsid was released the following month.

> *I was in prisons jails cutting grass with hoes*
> *Judges torturers blanks clouds funerals*
> *I have tried to be as coherent as possible*
> *Speech forgetting memory weakness disappear*
> *If you live in Juba you can't say I haven't tried*
> *Airports churches classes hospitals shops noticeboards*
> *If you can't read my meaning it is all your fault*
> *Words secrets writing daylight darkness*
> *My mind was deranged in the torture*
> *Bulbs light electricity testicles currents swoonings*
> *I am pulling myself together through the power of speech*
>
> Taban Lo Liyong from the poem *Clouds, Accounts, Gods etc.*
> Reproduced with permission of Zimbabwe Publishing House (PVT) Ltd. Harare

2

The apparatus of repression

"Beware of the tears of orphans and the prayers of those who are victimized."
Lieutenant Colonel Mustapha Ahmad Hassan al-Tai, on trial in Khartoum, January 1994

The authorities have routinely used detention without charge or trial, often involving torture and ill-treatment, to silence real or suspected political opponents. The security services are responsible for arresting and holding political detainees. Some detainees, notably military personnel suspected of plotting coups, have been brought to trial. Procedures in military trials have been clearly unfair; since the purging of the civilian judiciary there is also concern that political trials following normal judicial procedures have also been unfair.

A legal veneer

The government has attempted to give a legal veneer to the pattern of repression. In 1990 it passed a National Security Act (NSA) which created a National Security Council and Bureau. The act gives security officers powers of arrest and detention for interrogation, as well as powers of entry and search. In June 1991 the legislation was amended to bring detention without charge or trial, which under the 1990 act could be for an indefinite period and not subject to periodic review, under judicial control. Even if the State of Emergency is eventually lifted, the authorities have, through the NSA, invested the security services with extensive powers to suppress the slightest opposition to the government.

Under current legislation the security services are entitled to detain a person for interrogation, without access to families or lawyers, for periods of 72 hours renewable up to one month. "Preventive detention" for the "maintenance of public security", authorized by the Security Council, is allowed for periods not exceeding three months — unless the Security Council, or its authorized representative, allows an extension for a further three months. Such decisions have to be approved by a magistrate. Detainees are to be informed of the reasons for their detention "at an appropriate time" after their detention. "Bodily hurt" and "savage treatment" are forbidden.

Detainees can appeal against non-compliance with the detention regulations to a magistrate who "may, after summary consideration, issue such an order as he may deem fit, for alleviation of the grievance". If a magistrate releases a prisoner, or if a prisoner who has served a jail sentence is released, that person can only be redetained after a lapse of one month "or upon the permission of a magistrate".

These regulations appear to contain some safeguards of detainees' rights, but these are illusory and have not prevented arbitrary incommunicado detention and torture. The regulations fall far short of international standards. The hearings that are provided for are summary and detainees only have the right to challenge their detention before a magistrate when the authorities opt to extend the period of detention. They do have the right to petition the Security Council, the body responsible for authorizing the detention, but this does not constitute an independent judicial review, as required by international standards.

The repeated purging of officials in the Attorney General's offices and the judiciary means that Sudan's legal system is no longer independent of the government. The limited possibilities of review by magistrates do not amount to an appeal to an impartial judicial body. Amnesty International does not know of a single case in which a detainee has been able to appeal against non-compliance with detention regulations or against ill-treatment. The authorities claim this indicates that human rights violations are not taking place. However, former detainees have testified that they were not able to challenge their detention or the treatment they were receiving.

Torture and ill-treatment

Torture and ill-treatment are endemic in security service detention. Routine beatings, harsh regimes of physical exercise or prolonged exposure to the sun appear to be regarded as normal methods of dealing with prisoners.

CHAPTER 2

In April 1992 Amnesty International published testimony from prisoners who had been detained in Khartoum during July 1991 describing torture and ill-treatment at both the security headquarters and "ghost houses".[1] The detainees described beatings before being questioned, the application of hot metal to skin, being made to roll on hot, gritty surfaces and being made to stand completely still for up to 24 hours at a time.

Detainees were transferred to "ghost houses" in ways which prevented them learning where they were being taken; these included being forced under the seats of a minibus and being made to lie on the back of a pick-up truck covered with a blanket and then driven at speed around Khartoum streets. At the "ghost house" they were met by so-called "reception committees" who beat them before confining them in overcrowded cells. The "ghost house" regime included various forms of ill-treatment known as *idara dakhlia* (internal administration), apparently based on disciplinary methods within the armed forces, which included various forms of physical contortion or repetitive exercise.

The government dis-

Most political detainees are held in harsh conditions in so-called "ghost houses" run by the security services.

'THE TEARS OF ORPHANS'

missed these reports out of hand. However, prisoners detained in subsequent years describe almost identical ill-treatment. A journalist detained for eight months in 1992 has described being tortured after security officers ransacked his house and discovered a list of names of men executed in April 1990, among them his brother-in-law. The journalist and a friend arrested with him were taken to the security headquarters where they were registered and then blindfolded, forced into the back of a car face down and driven for a long time around Khartoum:

> "We stopped at about 3pm, a gate was opened and we drove through. We were dragged from the car, told to stand against a wall with our hands up and against it, then we were struck by many people all over our bodies with electric cable, plastic water pipes, and lengths of wood. This lasted from 3pm until 8pm — with an interruption at 6pm for evening prayers...this is referred to as the 'reception party'.
>
> "At around 11pm, I was blindfolded and taken...to an unknown destination...they said I should make a will. They told me I was going to be pushed down a well and they took me to the brink of some kind of space. When I was pushed I was ready for a long fall but the floor was only about one metre down. I lost consciousness.
>
> "Then I was...forced up some stairs and made to lie on what felt like a leather couch. After a few seconds I began to feel small but painful cuts all over my body, as if they were made by razor blades. This went on for around two hours with some breaks. Afterwards I was covered in small wounds. I was taken back to the 'ghost house' around 3am.
>
> "This pattern of being made to stand all night, sometimes being taken to the other place for the 'couch treatment' and sometimes just being taken outside and kicked and beaten continued until the next Wednesday, six days after my arrest."

The journalist was then moved, blindfold, apparently to another "ghost house". On arrival he was again beaten and kicked:

> "Twelve of us were made to lie on the ground and roll while being beaten. They sprayed the ground with water so that it became muddy. The other 12 were made to do 'squat jumps' like rabbits. There was another torture called sitt

CHAPTER 2

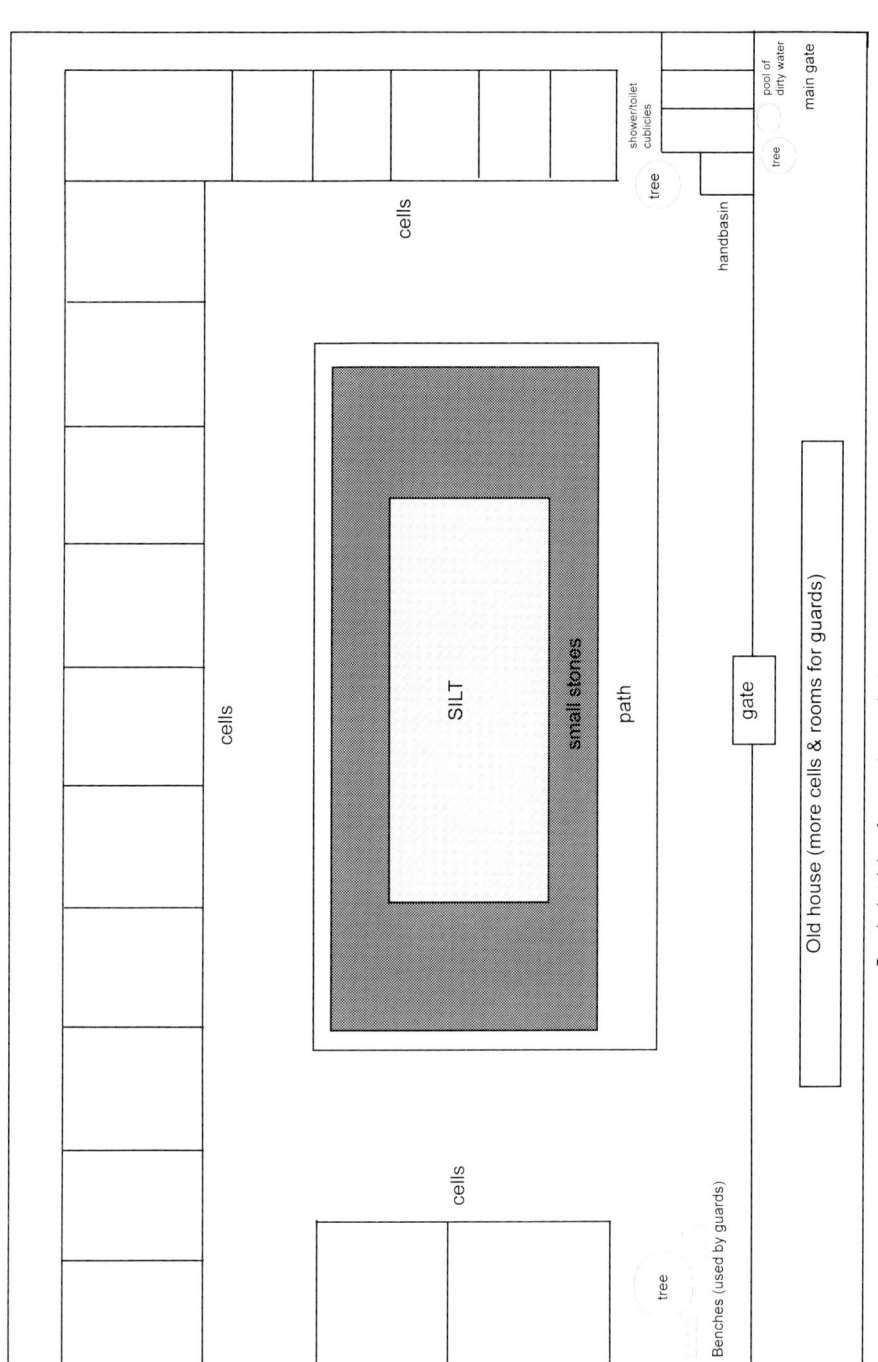

Rough sketch by a former prisoner of a "ghost house" in east Khartoum

'THE TEARS OF ORPHANS'

al-aragi. *They make you put your left hand to your right ear and put your right arm through the loop made by the left. Then, with your right forefinger on the ground and your legs straight you run in a circle round your finger. If you walk they beat you.*

"*The next morning...they brought in the poet al-Tijani Hussein Daffala al-Sid. He was bleeding badly all over. The middle finger-nail of his right hand had been pulled out and he had a wound in his cheek below his right eye. He was made to join the session. He quickly fell unconscious.*"

Deaths in detention

The harsh regime of torture and ill-treatment in "ghost houses" and security offices has led to a number of deaths, none of which has been properly investigated. The first recorded death was that of Ali Fadul, a doctor active in the suspended Doctors' Union, in April 1990. An official autopsy, reportedly carried out without the presence of a pathologist, gave malaria as the cause of death. His family were told he had died of cerebral meningitis. The family demanded another autopsy. After judicial intervention, this took place on 22 April and reportedly indicated that death was caused by a cerebral haemorrhage caused by a heavy blow. The security authorities refused to release the body for burial and instead buried it themselves during the curfew.

The family made three attempts to file a complaint against named security officials. The first was rejected by a judge as groundless. The second, to the offices of the Attorney General, was ignored. Following the third attempt, a judge ruled that the family should be given access to certain police and medical records. The judge was retired by the authorities and the lawyer assisting the family had his licence to practice revoked. In a response to the UN Special Rapporteur in February 1994, the authorities continued to insist that Ali Fadul died of "a severe attack of malaria".

There have since been other suspicious deaths in detention. In November 1991 Mehdi Mohamed Ahmad, agent for the Shell Petroleum company in Bara, died reportedly after being beaten by security officers who suspected him of hoarding fuel. In June 1992 the body of Mohamed Abdalla 'Abd al-Magid was reportedly found dumped by a road in Omdurman, three months after he had been taken into detention. In April 1994 Nadir Abdel Hamid Khairy, who had been in incommunicado detention since December 1993, died in Omdurman Military Hospital, apparently after prolonged serious beatings. The authorities refused to release the body to his family. In September 1994 Abdelmoneim Rahama, a trade unionist from Wad Medani, died in custody after being denied medical treatment for malaria.

Sexual abuse

Some former detainees have alleged that their torture has involved either the threat of or actual sexual abuse. In July 1990 a detainee held in Kober Prison wrote a petition of complaint to the Minister of Interior in which he alleged that while held at the security headquarters in Khartoum in June 1990 he was threatened with sodomy. Other detainees have described being stripped and then verbally humiliated. Some have described having their testicles crushed by pliers or being stabbed in their genitals by pins or screwdrivers.

Rape, whether of women or men, is regarded as a degradation almost beyond articulation in Sudan. In August 1993 Brigadier Mohamad Ahmad al-Rayah al-Faki, then held in Suakin civil prison, wrote a petition to the Minister of Justice in which he alleged that after his arrest in August 1991 on suspicion of involvement in a coup attempt he was raped by security men while being tortured in the security headquarters in Khartoum. He also described being "sexually abused by solid objects", the crushing of his testicles by pliers, receiving electric shocks from cattle prods around his genitals, as well as beatings and other forms of torture. The letter was smuggled out of Sudan and received extensive publicity. In November 1993 the authorities announced that a judicial investigation into the allegations was under way, but no report of this investigation has been published.

Torture as policy

The authorities deny that torture and ill-treatment are official policy and point out that they are crimes under both the penal code and the NSA. The *Sudan document on human rights*, which sets out the government's own human rights philosophy, contains a ringing denunciation of torture. The government asserts that detainees have the formal right under the law to submit complaints to the judicial authorities and that allegations of systematic torture are merely propaganda by the political opposition.

The official denial that torture is systematic is at odds with the testimony from dozens of former prisoners who have been held in "ghost houses" or the security headquarters at different times. Equally damning is the testimony of prisoners that torture takes place with the full knowledge, and sometimes in the presence, of the highest officials in the security services.

The authorities have sometimes claimed that they have investigated allegations of torture. In February 1993 the Minister of Justice and Attorney General, defending Sudan's human rights record at the UN Commission on Human Rights in Geneva, announced that 11 security officers had been tried after they had been accused of torturing detainees. He did not announce when these trials had taken place or what the verdicts of the court had been, with the exception of a death sentence passed on a security officer from Sennar.

However, given the regularity and consistency of reports of torture, the official reaction is inconsistent not only with the government's obligations under international standards to investigate such reports, but also with its obligations under the UN's 1975 Declaration on the Protection of All Persons Being Subjected to Torture to take effective steps to prevent torture, even if complaints are rarely submitted through official channels. There are two possible reasons for the lack of official action. The first is that the security services operate beyond the control of those parts of the political establishment which might wish to curb their worst excesses. The former chairman of the TNA human rights committee has reported that the committee's investigations of human rights violations were always blocked by the security services. The second, given the close interrelationship of the security services and the most powerful elements in the political establishment, is that the political authorities themselves condone or do not wish to know about the abuses.

Unfair trials

Some political prisoners have been brought to trial. The parallel special court system created after the coup, while the authorities were purging the judiciary, was notoriously unfair. The demise of certain special courts in 1991 removed one arena for human rights

CHAPTER 2

Twenty-eight army officers were executed in April 1990 24 hours after they were arrested and accused of mounting a coup.

abuse. However, political prisoners in Sudan have also been convicted at unfair trials in both military and civilian courts. The creation of a compliant judiciary means that political prisoners are at risk of unfair trial wherever they are tried.

Unfair trials in military courts

In April 1990 the authorities announced that they had foiled an attempted coup. Scores of soldiers were arrested and 24 hours later, on 24 April, 28 army officers were executed after a trial at which they had no legal representation. Two of the men executed were reportedly arrested at least three days before the alleged coup attempt; some sources claim that they were executed before the date of the trial. There are reports that between 60 and 90 soldiers from other ranks were also executed around the same time.

In September 1990, 13 civilians and 28 non-commissioned officers from southern Sudan and the Nuba mountains were arrested on suspicion of plotting a coup. In December 1990 the 13 civilians were tried before a military tribunal at which they were not allowed legal representation or to call defence witnesses. The

33

'THE TEARS OF ORPHANS'

Al-Hajj 'Abd al-Rahman Abdallah Nugdalla, a prominent member of the Umma Party and former government minister, who is serving a prison sentence of 10 years after he was convicted at an unfair trial of involvement in a coup plot.

trials lasted only a few minutes. One man was acquitted, but remained in detention for a further 10 months. Eleven of the 28 non-commissioned officers were reportedly sentenced to death, which was commuted to life imprisonment. The others were sentenced to prison terms.

In August 1991 the authorities arrested more than 80 civilians and serving and former army officers and announced they had foiled yet another coup plot. Many of those detained were held in the security headquarters and "ghost houses" in Khartoum, and tortured. On 11 October, 53 of the prisoners were tried before three specially convened military tribunals. The trials were held at night while a curfew was in force and were thus effectively held *in camera*. The sentences were not made known until early December, when film of the trial was shown on Sudanese television. It was announced that 11 prisoners had received death sentences, which were commuted to life imprisonment. Another 35 received sentences of up to 20 years' imprisonment.

In July 1992 the authorities announced an amnesty for prisoners sentenced to up to 15 years' imprisonment for crimes related to state security. An army spokesperson later said that 60 army officers and more than 50 civilians were set free. However, the actual number of people freed remains unclear. The official list named 59 people. Nineteen prisoners sentenced to more than 20 years had their sentences commuted to 10 years' imprisonment. Among those who remained in jail were al-Hajj 'Abd al-Rahman Abdallah Nugdalla, a prominent member of the Umma Party, and Brigadier Mohamad Ahmad al-Rayah al-Faki. In a press conference on 27 July 1992 announcing the amnesty, the Minister of Justice and Attorney General is reported to have said that the decree "has closed the door before those who had alleged that justice was not adhered to during trials".

In February 1994, in a response to a report by the UN Special Rapporteur to the Commission on Human Rights, the authorities said that military officers "who attempted to overthrow the legitimate government by force [in 1990 and 1991]" had been charged and tried before properly convened courts-martial. The government said that at such courts-martial the accused has the right to be "assisted in his defence during the trial by a legal adviser, or any other person of his choice". However, according to the testimony of defendant after defendant in different military trials, none was allowed proper legal representation or was able to call defence witnesses. According to the government, sentences in military tribunals are subject "to appeal or review before higher judicial bodies which are entitled to cancel, amend or confirm them". There is provision within the People's Armed Forces Act for a Military Court of Appeal constituted on the assent of the Head of State. This, however, is an *ad hoc* court which lacks any guarantee of judicial independence or impartiality. Indeed, no such tribunal heard an appeal for the 28 officers executed in April 1990 and there is no evidence that the cases of other defendants in other military trials were ever taken to an appeal court.

Unfair trials in civilian courts

The civilian court system appears to contain a number of safeguards guaranteeing fair trial. However, the actual fairness of these courts has been severely undermined by the creation of a judiciary which is compliant with the government's wishes.

The trial in early 1994 of 29 men, 17 *in absentia*, on various charges relating to conspiracy to cause explosions was one of the first high-profile political trials after the coup.[2] It was held in

'THE TEARS OF ORPHANS'

Khartoum, in a special court convened according to the regulations governing normal High Court procedures. The 12 men present in the court-room were arrested in April and May 1993. The defence team included several prominent lawyers, many of whom had spent periods in detention and one of whom, Ali Mahmud Hassanein, was detained for two weeks after the trial.

In April 1994 five of the defendants in the court-room were sentenced to prison terms ranging from two to seven years. The others present were freed. During the trial detailed evidence emerged, supported by official medical reports requested by the court, that at least five of the accused had been forced to confess after being tortured. The weight of the prosecution case rested on these confessions.

The testimony to the court of al-Hassan Ahmad Saleh, a tax inspector in Khartoum sentenced to two years' imprisonment, is harrowing. He describes being interrogated by two of the most senior security commanders in Sudan as officers struck him repeatedly with whips and sticks:

> "They took me to an office where they showed me the things they supposedly found in my house. I told them I knew nothing about it...They took me outside and made me stand under the sun for a long time while they beat me up. Then three security men told me to lie down on the ground. When I refused they started beating me with sticks and hoses until they got me to obey. This went on for some time while my hands were tied. Then they told me to stand under the sun again, barefoot and almost naked. Then, while they beat me from head to toe, my left eye was badly injured. I completely lost my sight in that eye...I thought I was going to die...especially because they threatened me with [death].
>
> "They continued to beat me up till the afternoon when they took me to the deputy security commander. He told me that he had been informed of my eye injury and told me that he would not have me treated, even if I lost the eye, unless I admitted to what they wanted me to. They took me back to a room and I was tied standing up to the door till the morning.
>
> "...They went on torturing me despite my eye injury...they took us by car to another house. They lined us against the wall while the soldiers went round each of us

CHAPTER 2

one at a time asking whether we had heard of 'ghost houses'. They then said that this was a 'ghost house', a place of torture. Then we were taken into cells and tied to the door for 15 days from 10pm until morning prayers.

"On 8 May they said they were going to show me hell that night. They took me out of the cell and one of the guards [tortured me] until I fainted. It was then that someone came with a hot iron and threatened that if I did not confess [the iron would be applied to my body]...so I ended up saying what they wanted me to when I was questioned."

The judge, despite acknowledging that at least five of the men had been tortured, decided that this did not disqualify the confessions. This is contrary to international standards and to the principles of Islamic jurisprudence. There are serious doubts about the fairness of the convictions.

*Sudan is so diverse
in culture and religion
with myriad ethnic colours
that those who do believe
in ultimate security
and economic solvency
should pin their hopes on peace
for force will not relieve.*

*Sudan has paid
a high price for wars
and destruction
It has become a wasteland
its very core flawed
Its sons are displaced
dispersed without slumber
Some had to flee abroad
a trip of no return, they vowed.*

A.M. Zein from the poem *The Wound of the South*
Reproduced with author's permission

3
'National Salvation'

"A National Salvation Revolution has taken place to rescue Sudan's image from that of a country being an incarnation of failure, corruption and instability, and its reputation of being linked with poverty, starvation, displacement, expatriation, humiliation and beggary."

Lieutenant-General Omar Hassan Ahmad al-Bashir, in a speech marking the first anniversary of the 30 June 1989 coup

Measures taken to restore Sudan's image include clearing displaced people from squatter camps in and around the capital and rounding up "street-children". This has directly affected more than one million of Sudan's poorest citizens.

The moral reorientation of Sudanese society along the lines of the government's interpretation of Islam has affected virtually the entire population of northern Sudan. Central to this is the imposition of a penal code based on the government's interpretation of Islamic law. To many Sudanese the existence of a penal code based on an interpretation of *Shari'a* law is deeply contentious, not only to non-Muslims, mainly southerners who make up approximately one third of the population, but also to many Muslim northern Sudanese.

The authorities have stipulated that, as yet, the system of retribution (*qisas*) in punishment for certain offences and the *hudud* provisions within the penal code — provisions which derive from interpretations of Islamic law, for example those relating to drinking and dealing in alcohol, and others which define offences such as apostasy (*riddah*), grand theft punishable by amputation (*sariqah hadiyah*), extra-marital sex (*zina*) and the false accusation of inchastity (*qazf*) — do not apply in southern Sudan. However, many non-Muslim southerners resident in northern Sudan feel

'THE TEARS OF ORPHANS'

Shilluk displaced from the war zones in Upper Nile living in a squatter camp in Khartoum. The displaced are in an appalling position. The government sees them as a social and economic problem and is forcibly resettling them away from the capital. © *Jeremy Hartley/Panos*

culturally discriminated against by the Islamic penal code.

Amnesty International takes no position on the government's political aims or its ideology. Neither does Amnesty International take a position on the appropriate basis of law for Sudan or any other country. Its concerns arise when the implementation of the government's program results in human rights violations. Certain provisions within the penal code, notably those providing for the punishments of flogging and amputation, constitute cruel, inhuman or degrading punishments under international standards.

Dealing with the displaced

When the government took power in 1989, Khartoum and other northern cities were host to more than a million southern and western Sudanese, many of them non-Muslim, displaced from areas afflicted by conflict or famine. Most were women, children and the elderly. Camps for displaced people surrounded the capital; people lived in rough shelters of sacking and cardboard erected on wasteland and even on rubbish dumps. Some had become

CHAPTER 3

well-established, building mud-brick houses in areas around the city's fringes.

Most of the settlement was unlicensed and thus technically illegal. Uneducated and predominantly of rural background, many of the displaced found getting formal employment in Khartoum difficult. Many women supported themselves by petty trading or brewing; some by begging or prostitution. Large numbers have been arrested and publicly flogged as a result.

The displaced are in an appalling position. The government sees them as a social and economic problem and has tried to resettle them outside Khartoum. In August 1989, publicly stressing that all relocation was on a voluntary basis, the government began forced relocations with the destruction of houses in squatter camps around Khartoum. The scale of official action intensified in 1990. Tens of thousands were relocated in 1991. "Transit" camps were established in Jebel Aulia, 40 kilometres south of Khartoum, and in a dry and wind-swept site 12 kilometres west of Omdurman. Non-governmental organizations reported that these camps were ill-prepared and grossly inadequate. By late 1992 more than 700,000 people had been moved out of the capital. The homes of a further 160,000 people were demolished between August 1993 and July 1994; in July alone 60,000 people were reported to have been forcibly moved.

Relocations are often accompanied by force, or the threat of force. More than 20 people have been killed as bulldozers accompanied by police and security forces have burned and destroyed shelters and houses. In some situations riots have ensued as shanty town dwellers have tried to defend their homes. In others the sudden ferocity of demolition raids by the authorities, sometimes at night, has led to chaos and loss of life.

Rounding up street children

The growth in the numbers of displaced people in Sudan has been matched by the growth in the number of children living on the streets of Khartoum. Official figures state that there are more than 25,000 vagrant children in and around Khartoum. In September 1992 the Khartoum authorities initiated a program to remove vagrant children from the streets. Since then a series of special camps and schools have been created.

The authorities argue that the rounding-up of street children is a social welfare measure, designed to protect them from "the multiple risks and dangers confronting street children, including addiction, pornography, prostitution and sale of organs".[3] Whatever the intentions behind the policy, AI is concerned that children are being arbitrarily detained.

According to most independent sources, children are rounded up by the police in an arbitrary manner and are often held for some days in police stations before being taken to the special camps. The government claims that children who can give information about their parents are reunited with them. However, such information is not acted upon. Many southern Sudanese living in Khartoum now escort their children in public places to ensure they do not lose them to the authorities.

There are reports of police violence against children when they are being rounded up and of cruel, inhuman or degrading punishments, including flogging and being placed in leg-irons, for children who try to escape from the camps. Nineteen boys aged between three and 11 were rounded up at a market in Kalakala, a Khartoum suburb, in April 1993 and taken to a police station in Soba, south of Khartoum. On arrival at the police station they were accused of being thieves and were beaten. They were then taken to a special camp in Soba, which appears to act as a "clearing centre" where the children are interviewed before being allocated to other camps or schools. One child managed to escape. The others were then beaten. Four boys who tried to escape from a camp in June 1993 reported that after they were caught each was flogged and made to stand with his arms raised above his head with a brick in each hand.

Cruel, inhuman or degrading punishments

The Penal Code 1991 contains provisions for penalties which violate Sudan's treaty obligations under the International Covenant on Civil and Political Rights (ICCPR) and are inconsistent with international human rights law. These include the penalties of flogging and amputation, and provisions which allow for mutilation and death in retribution. These penalties existed in the 1983 penal code and Amnesty International has raised its concerns about them with each government in power in Sudan since then. Amnesty International is also concerned by the continuing use of the death penalty.

CHAPTER 3

A man receives 20 lashes from a police officer immediately after he was sentenced for drinking alcohol by a Public Order Court. © Abbas/Magnum

Flogging

Flogging constitutes a cruel, inhuman or degrading punishment and as such is specifically prohibited under international human rights law. Corporal punishment has a long history in Sudanese penal codes. The Penal Code introduced in March 1991 contains 18 sections defining a wide variety of offences which are punishable by flogging: prostitution is punishable by up to 100 lashes, wearing clothing contrary to public decency is punishable by up to 40 lashes and causing a breach of the peace is punishable by up to 20 lashes.

Thousands of sentences of flogging have been handed down by the courts, both the Magistrates Courts and Public Order Courts, since June 1989. Some of the victims have been middle-class Sudanese men suspected of political opposition to the government. In September 1992 Mohamed Mahjoub, a prominent lawyer in al-Fasher, in western Sudan, who had defended political prisoners arrested in Darfur, received 99 lashes after being arrested at a party in his home and convicted of drinking alcohol, gambling and consorting with prostitutes. There was reportedly no evidence that he was guilty. In November 1993 eight men, including the three brothers of a prominent human rights activist in exile, received 40

'THE TEARS OF ORPHANS'

lashes in Wad Medani after they had been convicted of drinking alcohol. Other prominent citizens who have been flogged include Peter al-Birish, an Anglican bishop, who received 80 lashes in Khartoum in July 1993, after he had been convicted of extra-marital sex.

Hundreds of those flogged have been women, many of them poor and from the displaced population in and around major cities. Many displaced southern women brew and sell alcohol as a way of supporting themselves and their families in the squatter camps. Strictly within the terms of the law non-Muslims who make or sell alcohol are not liable to be flogged, but there are many reports of women being flogged for alcohol-related offences. In one three-day period in early 1993, seven non-Muslim women, two of whom were pregnant, were given 40 lashes each for brewing alcohol in al-Mayo squatter settlement in Khartoum. There were further reports of

It is an offence to wear clothing defined as obscene or contrary to public morals. This has been particularly applied to women in whose case it is interpreted to mean that in public their hair should be covered and the attire should be sufficiently loose and opaque to conceal the shape of the body. Women who do not conform are at risk of being flogged. © *Hutchison*

CHAPTER 3

floggings in mid-1994 after the Khartoum State authorities announced a campaign to eradicate the brewing and drinking of alcohol. In the first 16 days of June 1994, 657 people were charged with alcohol-related offences.

Additionally, specific offences within the penal code, and provisions within certain by-laws, for example those which define standards of dress, have been interpreted in ways which particularly affect women and have led to their being flogged. The Penal Code 1991 does not define any particular form of dress, but Section 152 defines the offence of wearing an outfit that is obscene or contrary to public morals. This is open to wide interpretation. In December 1991 the Governor of Khartoum put forward general guidelines for women which included keeping the hair and body covered and ensuring the attire is sufficiently loose and opaque to conceal the shape of the body. Trousers or buttoned shirts uncovered by a long loose garment are not regarded as appropriate. Additionally, women should not wear perfume, jewellery or cosmetics. Although the terms of Section 152 are ambiguous about whether it applies to non-Muslims, and some non-Muslims have been convicted under it, it has been particularly applied to Muslim women.

These dress standards have been enforced in several ways. These include encouraging citizens to report women who do not conform and requiring women to be appropriately dressed before they can get access to government services. In January 1991 women working in government departments were ordered to wear "appropriate" dress. In February 1994 the Ministry of Education announced that female Muslim students must cover all parts of their body except the face and hands.

Women not conforming to the dress code have been flogged. A non-Muslim woman living in Omdurman was fined and sentenced to 35 lashes after being arrested in late 1991 for wearing trousers and brought before a Public Order Court:

> *"I paid them their fine but I refused to take the lashes. So at once the judge called a policeman from outside who took his whip and suddenly lashed me on my back. I was boiling with anger so I reacted badly. I grabbed the whip and twisted it. Then two or three policemen grabbed me and tied my hands to my back...they lashed me with my hands tied to my back.*

'THE TEARS OF ORPHANS'

> *"Before they finished I was crying and shouting 'Jesus'. At once the judge stopped the man from lashing and asked me, 'Why did you say Jesus? Is this a church for you to say Jesus?...This is not the place of Christians. You must not say Jesus again'. Then he said: 'Add on another five lashes.'*
>
> *"After I received 40 lashes, because I was angry, I gave him a venomous look. He noticed and gave me another five lashes."*

Students have also been arrested and flogged. In December 1992 a student at al-Ahfad University for women in Omdurman was flogged for wearing trousers. In late December 1993 a student at Khartoum University wearing a blouse and skirt was stopped by a guard outside her hall of residence and told to change her clothes. She refused and was taken to a Public Order Court where she received 25 lashes.

Women who do not conform to the dress code risk arrest on suspicion of other offences connected with public morality which are also punishable by flogging. In late 1991 a non-Muslim Ethiopian woman working as a domestic servant in Gereif was arrested while on an errand for her employers, on suspicion that she was a prostitute. The officer was alone and in plain clothes so she resisted the arrest because she suspected he might have been seeking to abduct and rape her. She reported being held overnight at a police station with 15 other women arrested while trying to get transport home. They were subjected to verbal abuse and humiliation by the police officers. At the Public Order Court next day they were all accused of being prostitutes:

> *"The judge, when he came, just took our names one by one. And after that he gave 40 lashes for each. He did not advise us, he did not even ask us the reasons we were there. He just sat down for some time, he took our names and after that he gave 40 lashes each. And we saw that the policemen who were looking through the doors, through the windows, were laughing at us."*

Amputation and other forms of mutilation

The first Sudanese penal code to include judicial amputation as a penalty was introduced in September 1983 by the government of Gaafar Nimeiri, and known as the "September Laws". Between

CHAPTER 3

Criminal prisoners in leg-irons in Kober Prison, 1994. © *Mark Stucci*

October 1983 and April 1985, when the government was overthrown in a military coup, more than 140 amputations were carried out. The "September Laws" remained in force until the Penal Code 1991 was introduced. Although after April 1985 the courts continued to impose sentences of judicial amputation under the "September Laws", the sentences do not appear to have been carried out.

Certain sections of the Penal Code 1991 also provide for amputation as a judicial penalty. Sections 167 and 168 define the offence of highway robbery (*haraba*) and applicable punishments which include execution or execution followed by crucifixion if the offence involved murder or rape, and by amputation of the right hand and left foot if the offence involved inflicting grievous bodily harm or the theft of a sufficient amount. Sections 170 and 171 define grand theft (*sariqah hadiyah*) and the applicable punishment of amputation of the right hand. The standard defining the amount to qualify a theft as *sariqah hadiyah* is the value of a gold unit weighing 4.25 grammes.

In September 1993 the official spokesperson for the judiciary announced that the courts had been applying *hudud* punishments without making the verdicts public. It is unclear whether this referred to the sentencing of people to judicial amputation or to the carrying-out of sentences. Amnesty International is aware of two sentences of right-hand amputation imposed in Sennar on 5 Sep-

'THE TEARS OF ORPHANS'

Both the penal code and regulations governing the armed forces provide for the death penalty. Prisoners sentenced to death in civilian courts are liable to be hanged. Other methods of execution include stoning to death and execution by firing squad. © Mark Stucci

tember 1991 and a sentence of cross-limb (right hand and left foot) amputation imposed in al-Fasher on 19 September 1991 but does not know if they have been implemented. However, it appears that some sentences have been carried out. In May 1994 the Director of the Sudan Prisons Service confirmed in an interview that amputations had been carried out in Kober Prison, in Khartoum.

The Penal Code 1991 also provides for *qisas*, the right of relatives to choose that a deliberate offender be punished in the same manner as his or her act, in certain cases of murder or grievous bodily harm.

The UN Special Rapporteur on torture in his 1986 report concluded:

"Corporal punishments as 'lawful sanctions' under domestic laws may constitute 'severe pain or suffering' under international law. Consequently, this kind of chastisement should be revised in order to prevent torture, particularly amputations, caning or flogging."[4]

In his report to the Fiftieth Session of the UN Commission on Human Rights in early 1994, the UN Special Rapporteur on Sudan drew attention to these provisions within the law which he argued were

CHAPTER 3

"radically opposed to provisions of the international conventions to which the Sudan is a party".[5] The government responded by accusing him of attacking Islam.

The death penalty

The death penalty exists for a variety of offences including waging war against the state, apostasy, murder and rape outside marriage.[6] With some exceptions, hanging is the normal method of execution for persons convicted under the penal code. The exceptions are after conviction of *haraba* involving murder or rape in which case the convict is hanged until dead and his or her body then crucified; and after conviction of *zina* in marriage, in which case the execution is by stoning. In cases of murder the right of *qisas* exists. For persons convicted of offences defined in the Armed Forces Act 1986, such as mutiny, execution is normally by firing-squad.

Until they were disbanded in 1991 the various special courts handed down death sentences in several criminal cases involving persons accused of embezzlement, currency smuggling and drug-dealing. At least four men were executed after conviction in special courts. For example, the pilot Giorgis Yustus was sentenced to death in December 1989 for currency smuggling. He was executed in February 1990. He, like others convicted in the special courts, was sentenced after a summary hearing and did not have the right to lodge an appeal. Soldiers and civilians sentenced to death in military courts do not have the right of appeal either.

The High Court has also sentenced people to death and some have been executed. In 1991 at least 14 people convicted of criminal offences were hanged. One, Ibrahim Dubara Mongho, was executed and his body crucified in al-Fasher in western Sudan; he had been convicted of killing 20 people and stealing camels, horses and cattle in a raid on a village. In September 1994 a Libyan national convicted of murdering 16 people in a machine-gun attack on a mosque in February was hanged in Khartoum.

In recent years many prisoners sentenced to death for alleged political crimes have had their sentences commuted to imprisonment. In December 1991 death sentences on 11 men convicted of attempting a coup were commuted to terms of imprisonment. Retired Brigadier Nasr Hassan Nasr, a former diplomat at the Sudanese Embassy in Saudi Arabia, also benefited from a commutation. He was arrested in December 1991 and in May 1992 was convicted of espionage at a military trial. In February 1993 the sentence was commuted to life imprisonment. In September 1994 the death sentence against another man convicted of involvement in the February 1994 attack on the mosque was commuted to 10 years' imprisonment.

Amnesty International opposes the death penalty in all circumstances as a violation of the right to life and the right not to be subjected to cruel, inhuman or degrading treatment or punishment. The organization therefore welcomes these and other commutations of death sentences. However, Amnesty International remains concerned that the penalty still exists in law, that the courts continue to hand down death sentences and that executions still take place in Sudan.

The leaving of the old destroys my home
My bones sleep in the forest
Malou's absence destroys my home
My bones become white
My father has gone
Who will hold my life?

Agar Dinka song

4

The destruction of the south

Nearly three million people are displaced from their homes in southern Sudan. They are congregated around towns and cities, around feeding centres established by the UN and humanitarian organizations and in refugee camps in neighbouring countries. Whole communities have moved on to their neighbours' lands with a resulting increase in social conflict.

The war is being fought in southern Sudan and adjacent areas of the north such as the Nuba mountains, southern Blue Nile province and Darfur. All parties to the conflict have been ruthless in their assaults on civilians. These attacks are not the simple by-products of war but the result of a policy of killing non-combatants, driving them from their land and looting and destroying their means of livelihood. The attacks have created a humanitarian disaster.

Government forces seeking to destabilize or regain control of areas held by the armed opposition have deliberately targeted the rural population and the camps of displaced people. Such attacks have involved ground forces from the army and militia, both the PDF and ethnically based paramilitary groups. In the Nuba mountains whole communities have been forcibly relocated to so-called "peace villages" controlled by the army and PDF in areas outside the war zone.

Both of the main rebel factions, SPLA-Mainstream led by Dr John Garang de Mabior and SPLA-United led by Dr Riek Machar Teny-Dhurgon, have similarly assaulted civilians in bitter internecine warfare. These attacks have involved the deliberate pitting of one community against another, creating a cycle of revenge.

The extraordinarily high cost of the war in civilian deaths and destroyed communities is

'THE TEARS OF ORPHANS'

An air-raid drill at Palataka school near the Ugandan border in the far south of Sudan. Civilian targets have been regularly bombed.
© *Crispin Hughes/Panos*

difficult to quantify because there are no reliable statistics. The most comprehensive study of the available data estimates that more than 1.3 million people have died between the start of the war in May 1983 and May 1993.[7] In 1994 the UN estimated that 2.4 million war-affected persons would need emergency food aid during the year, and 5.2 million war-affected people would need non-food aid.[8]

The cost in civilian lives is only one dimension of the chronic failure to respect human rights. Each party to the conflict routinely murders prisoners captured on the battlefield. The SPLA-Mainstream has detained prominent dissidents within its ranks. Many have been tortured and some deliberately killed. Little, if any, action has been taken against human rights violators by the government or either faction of the SPLA.

While massive human rights violations continue to be perpetuated, past human rights violations cannot be considered a closed book. Four successive governments have prosecuted the war and been responsible for the violation of human rights. Many of the officials, politicians and army officers currently in positions of responsibility served in senior positions in previous administrations. Others form the main democratic opposition to the military government. If Sudan is ever to enjoy a just and lasting peace, the issue of human rights violations must be seriously confronted by Sudanese from all political factions.

The roots of conflict

The current war began in 1983 but its origins lie deep in Sudanese history. The fear of political, economic and cultural domination by northern Sudan was widespread even before Sudan became independent in 1956. Civil war rapidly followed independence, pitching government forces against secessionist rebels known as the Anyanya. An estimated 500,000 died, most of them civilians. A peace agreement concluded in 1972 granted southern Sudan regional autonomy. The Nuba mountains remained administratively within the north.

Eleven years of unstable peace followed. Economic decline spread through north and south as world recession, dramatic rises in the price of oil and a major reduction in Middle Eastern investment and aid combined to expose the weakness of Sudan's economy. By the early 1980s Sudan was locked in a spiralling crisis of

'THE TEARS OF ORPHANS'

debt, mostly to western creditors and the International Monetary Fund. The government lurched from one political crisis to another, to which it responded with growing repression.

Meanwhile southern Sudanese factional interests fought for control of the southern regional government, creating deadlock in regional decision-making. In 1980 the central authorities imposed an interim military government on the south after a political crisis developed over demands for southern Sudan to be divided into three autonomous regions. Supporters of division saw it as a way of lessening the power of politicians from the Dinka and Nuer ethnic groups, the largest groups in the south, whom they accused of incompetence and corruption. Opponents saw it as a breach of the agreement ending the Anyanya war.

In 1978 the discovery of oil in and around the marshlands of Upper Nile transformed the economic potential of southern Sudan. In the febrile political atmosphere this led to immediate suspicions among southerners that southern Sudan would not be given a proper share of the resulting wealth.

Throughout 1981 increasing political tension in north and south led to the arrest of many hundreds of government opponents. In May 1982 a coalition of southern political interests seeking division won regional elections. In May 1983, the President, beset by increasing political opposition in the north, announced the division of the autonomous southern region into three.

As the division of the south was announced, army units in Bor and Pibor, mutinied and went to the bush. By July 1983 around 3,000 soldiers had deserted. The announcement, within two months, of the "September Laws" was regarded by many southerners as confirmation of their worst fears about northern Sudanese cultural domination. By the end of the year the SPLA had been formed under the leadership of former army officer Dr John Garang de Mabior and war broke out in earnest.

The place of religion in the war

Much of the rhetoric surrounding the war in Sudan characterizes it in terms of Arabs fighting Africans, northerners against southerners and Muslims at war with Christians. None of these simplifications accurately describes the complex political cleavages underlying the fighting.

The war is not just a southern war. Some of the most extensive human rights violations of the war have been perpetrated in the

CHAPTER 4

Nuba mountains, an area administratively outside southern Sudan and populated by around one million people, many of whom regard themselves as Africans. While a sense of racial discrimination by the central authorities fuels the grievances of many southerners and people claiming African origins from other parts of Sudan, there are people who identify themselves as Arab fighting with the SPLA and there are many southerners and Nuba fighting with the government.

The issue of religion is particularly emotive. Bigots on all sides, Muslims and Christians alike, have exploited religion, making it a significant factor in the continuing fighting. On the one hand the central authorities are seeking to effect the moral reorientation of Sudanese society. Measures towards this include imposing the Penal Code 1991, which is based on an interpretation of *Shari'a* (Islamic) law, in northern Sudan, and by implementing strict codes of public morality. Although the specific penalties and offences devised from Islamic jurisprudence are not applied in the south, to many southerners, especially those living in the north, the implementation of the Penal Code 1991 confirms their belief that they are viewed as second-class citizens by the government. The government expressly appeals to religious values by describing the war as a *jihad*, a holy war against unbelievers in Islam. On the other hand, supporters of the SPLA factions sometimes characterize their rebellion as being Christian resistance to the spread of Islam. There are, however, Muslims and Christians on both sides.

While the war cannot be reduced to issues of race or religion, racist attitudes and religious bigotry exert a real influence on the behaviour of some individuals in the war zones, including individuals in positions of power and influence over others. Issues of ethnicity and intolerance underlie some of the grossest human rights violations.

Human rights violations in the war zones

Both the military government which took power in 1985 and the civilian government which replaced it in 1986 pursued a policy of using proxy militia forces to fight the SPLA. This strategy first emerged in 1984 when the government of President Ga'afar Nimeiri forged links with Nuer-based rebels in Upper Nile, known as the Anyanya Two. In 1985 militia forces were raised from ethnic groups in Upper Nile and Equatoria. The militia were little more

'THE TEARS OF ORPHANS'

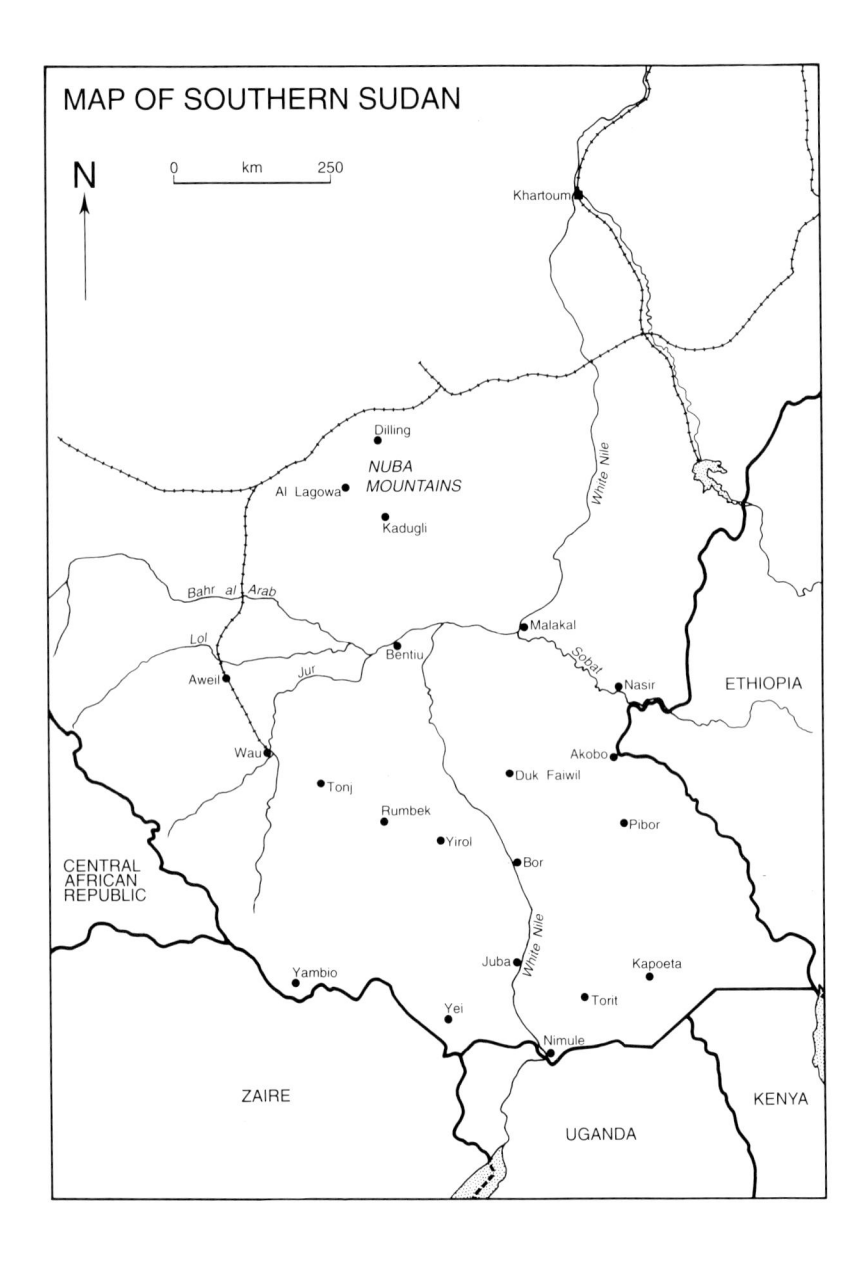

MAP OF SOUTHERN SUDAN

CHAPTER 4

than an ill-disciplined rabble, armed by the government, who supported themselves through looting with impunity. They were responsible for ruthless assaults on civilians from other ethnic communities and for killing members of their own communities thought to be SPLA supporters or hostile to the activities of the militia.

The advent of a civilian government in 1986 saw a dramatic intensification of human rights violations. The militia policy was extended. New forces were formed and were responsible for gross human rights violations. Throughout 1987 in Wau, the largest town in Bahr al-Ghazal, government troops and Fertit militia abducted and murdered hundreds of Dinka civilians. The killings reached a peak in August and September with the massacre of over 1,000 civilians in apparent reprisal for a missile attack on a military plane.

Until 1987 the most intense military activity took place in Upper Nile where the SPLA, with major bases located inside Ethiopia and backing from the Ethiopian Government, was locked in a bitter struggle with Anyanya Two. However, in late 1987 a significant proportion of the Anyanya Two joined the SPLA, which then consolidated its forces in Eastern Equatoria and pushed greater numbers of troops into the Nuba mountains and Bahr al-Ghazal.

Between 1985 and 1988 northern Bahr al-Ghazal was devastated by a series of raids by the *murahaleen*, a militia raised from the Rizeiqat and Misseriya nomadic tribes of Southern Darfur and Southern Kordofan. Initially self-armed, the *murahaleen* developed close links with the armed forces and the Umma Party, historically the strongest party in western Sudan. The raids, which involved the killing of thousands of Dinka civilians, rape, the abduction of women and children, the looting of livestock and the destruction of homesteads, led to severe famine in northern Bahr al-Ghazal and the displacement of hundreds of thousands of civilians, many of whom ended up squatting in shanty towns in and around Khartoum.

While the *murahaleen* were motivated more by securing access to dry-season pastures along the Bahr al-Arab river, historically shared with the Dinka, and by the prospect of looting cattle, than by national political considerations, the raids coincided with the military aim of destabilizing a population regarded as supporting the SPLA. There were widespread allegations of cooperation

'THE TEARS OF ORPHANS'

between army units and militia. The political authorities failed to intervene.

Meanwhile the armed forces were also responsible for torturing and killing civilians and captured prisoners on the battlefield in the war zones. In December 1986, 22 SPLA soldiers captured by government forces in Upper Nile were executed. In the Nuba mountains soldiers were responsible for scores of extrajudicial executions in 1987 and 1988. Agricultural labourers from the Dinka, Meban, Uduk and Shilluk peoples were arrested in late 1987 and early 1988 after the SPLA captured the town of Kurmuk in Blue Nile. Many were reportedly tortured and extrajudicially executed. All this occurred while a democratically elected government was in power, with relatively few human rights violations occurring in areas unaffected by the war.

When the military government came to power in 1989, the SPLA controlled most of southern Sudan; during the next two years the SPLA gained territory in Western Equatoria, Bahr al-Ghazal and along the Ethiopian border. Increasingly beleaguered government forces controlled the three major towns, Juba, Wau and Malakal, and a handful of smaller garrisons scattered across the south. SPLA control

Popular Defence Force soldiers are taught to use guns at a training camp near Khartoum. Students must undergo military training. Volunteers are sent to the war in the south. © *Abbas/Magnum*

CHAPTER 4

was weakest in the Nuba mountains, but even here government forces were largely confined to Kadugli and other small towns.

The current government has continued the strategy of using militia forces. The *murahaleen* were consolidated into the PDF, directly controlled by the military authorities. PDF troops have been repeatedly responsible for persistent gross human rights violations in the Nuba mountains. They have raided northern Bahr al-Ghazal and have been deployed to clear civilians from lands along both sides of the railway line connecting north and south, a vital military supply route for the government. In northern Bahr al-Ghazal and the Nuba mountains the PDF appear to have licence to kill with impunity.

In mid-1991 the Ethiopian Government collapsed and the SPLA lost its major arms supplier and the use of Ethiopia as a sanctuary. SPLA troops and hundreds of thousands of refugees fled Ethiopia into Upper Nile province. Among those fleeing were thousands of children who had been living in camps. Many were orphans, but others had been separated from their parents by the SPLA on the pretext that they would be educated. These "unaccompanied minors" eventually made their way to refugee camps in Kenya. It has been alleged that the SPLA has forcibly conscripted "unaccompanied minors" and other children.

Internal differences in the SPLA were accentuated by the crisis and in August 1991 SPLA commanders in Upper Nile split from the main body to form SPLA-Nasir, which later amalgamated with other SPLA dissident groups to form SPLA-United. Warfare between the two SPLA factions broke out almost immediately. This political division put the SPLA on the defensive, particularly in the isolated Nuba mountains, and opened up the south to government forces.

The government has made considerable military gains since late 1991, concentrating its effort against the SPLA-Mainstream. In early 1992 government forces recaptured the towns of Bor, Pochala, and Pibor in Upper Nile, Yirol in Bahr al-Ghazal, and the strategically important town of Torit in Eastern Equatoria. SPLA-Mainstream responded by tightening its siege of Juba, the major city in the south, which it almost captured that year. Following SPLA incursions into Juba in mid-1992, civilians and suspected deserters from the government side were extrajudicially executed by government forces and hundreds of people "disappeared".

In July 1993 the government began an offensive on the west bank of the White Nile in Eastern Equatoria, bombing civilian

'THE TEARS OF ORPHANS'

targets between Morobo and Yei and displacing some 75,000 people. In 1994 the government mounted a major assault on the east bank, aimed at securing the Ugandan border. In February over 100,000 people living in camps north of the border town of Nimule were forced to flee as government forces advanced. In June Kajo-Kaji, a town on the west bank of the Nile, was recaptured after many years in SPLA hands. Meanwhile, government forces were active in Bahr al-Ghazal between Tonj and Thiet. Civilians again appeared to be a primary target; government forces burned down each village they entered.

In the Nuba mountains the military government has followed a policy of forcibly clearing villages and resettling civilians in so-called "peace villages" under the control of the army and PDF. These attacks have involved extrajudicial executions, rapes and the abduction of women and children by militia forces.

The creation of humanitarian need

Since 1983, millions of rural people have become refugees in neighbouring countries or been displaced inside Sudan. Gross human rights violations, as much as natural disaster, have caused people to flee and reduced them to dependency upon famine foods gathered in the wild, and upon food relief provided mainly by the UN and non-governmental relief agencies. The story of the Uduk ethnic group starkly illustrates this.

In December 1986 the SPLA began operations in southern Blue Nile. The following year attacks by both government troops and Rufa'a militia on the non-Arab population of southern Blue Nile, whom the authorities regarded as SPLA supporters, led to the mass exodus of the Uduk. Approximately 25,000 Uduk fled to Ethiopia; many of those who did not flee were killed.

In December 1989 the Uduk refugee camp in Ethiopia was overrun by the Oromo Liberation Front (OLF), a rebel group fighting the Ethiopian Government, reportedly aided by Sudanese troops. The Uduk fled back to Sudan. On their way, the refugees were gunned down by OLF supporters, bombed by the Sudan air force and shelled by the army who suspected that SPLA soldiers were among them. Hundreds more died of starvation and disease during a 250-kilometre trek through Sudan to join hundreds of thousands of refugees in camps in Ethiopia's Gambella province.

Their sanctuary was short-lived. In June 1990, some 400,000 refugees, including the Uduk, returned to Sudan as security in

CHAPTER 4

A boy leads a blind old man. Millions of rural people have become refugees in foreign lands or displaced inside Sudan dependent on food relief provided, in the main, by the UN and non-governmental relief agencies.
© *David Stewart-Smith/Katz*

Gambella province deteriorated. They were bombed by the Sudan air force. The Uduk fled into SPLA territory and were settled on the lands of the Nuer ethnic group. Here they were harassed by SPLA soldiers.

In May 1992 the SPLA-Nasir faction agreed to relocate the Uduk around Kigille, east of Nasir. Once more they were harassed by SPLA soldiers who looted what little property they had. Parties of Uduk and other Blue Nile refugees tried to leave Kigille and return home. In mid-1992, two parties of several dozen set off; one group was ambushed by SPLA troops, the men were killed and the women and children abducted. Several thousand Uduk left Kigille and trekked to Itang in Ethiopia.

In July 1992 SPLA soldiers were among a large force of Nuer who attacked Itang and killed more than 200 highland Ethiopians. The Uduk fled further into Ethiopia.

For the moment, the surviving Uduk remain in a refugee camp in Gambella. In the past eight years they have trekked more than 1,000 kilometres, mostly on foot, in search of refuge from war. Those who survived did so primarily because of relief aid.

Killings and 'disappearances' in Juba

Extrajudicial executions and "disappearances" in Juba, the largest town in the south, followed two major assaults, in June and July 1992, by SPLA-Mainstream. They have a special significance in human rights terms. Most human rights violations by government forces take place in inaccessible garrison towns or remote rural areas. The Juba incidents took place in a major town in front of many eye-witnesses. These incidents give an indication of the probable military practice in places where there is even less chance that soldiers and the authorities will be held accountable for their actions.

During the SPLA assault, a number of government soldiers switched sides. As government forces regained control of the town, they responded by extrajudicially executing civilians and captured SPLA soldiers during house-to-house search operations, and arresting over 290 soldiers, police officers, prison guards, paramilitary forces attached to the Department of Wildlife and prominent civilians.[9] Around 80 of these people are reported to be in prison or to have been released. Most have "disappeared" and it is believed that the majority were summarily killed. The government has still not accounted for the "disappeared".

The incidents reported to Amnesty International include the killing of civilians as government troops moved from house to house through suburbs evacuated by the SPLA in search of SPLA soldiers. People who showed resistance and young adult men suspected of being SPLA soldiers were taken out and shot. People were killed in cold blood by soldiers who stopped them in the street. The day after the first SPLA attack, 40 soldiers providing air defence at Juba airport are known to have been extrajudicially executed.

The government claims that some of those arrested in Juba were brought before military tribunals. Nine prisoners are reported to have been sentenced to imprisonment. In September 1992 government officials admitted that Andrew Tombe, a Sudanese employee of the United States Agency for International Development and Mark Laboke Jenner, who worked for the European Commission, had been convicted of treason and had been executed in Juba in mid-August 1992.

In a few cases the government has either provided contradictory or false information about prisoners. In most cases it has

CHAPTER 4

provided no information at all. The "disappeared" include Kennedy Khamis, a customs official arrested in June 1992 after he went to Juba military headquarters in search of his missing son; and Joseph W. D. Wai, a geologist who returned to Sudan in late 1991 after studying for several years in the Netherlands. It is feared that both the 55 prisoners about whom the government has provided information and more than 150 others about whom the authorities have so far failed to provide any information have been executed, either extrajudicially or after summary hearings.

In November 1992, in the face of international protests and the threat of UN censure, the government established a committee chaired by a High Court judge to "investigate the incidents witnessed by Juba town in June and July". Because the terms of reference of this investigation were not well defined, it is not at all clear that allegations of human rights violations by agents of the state were the central part of this inquiry or even within its remit. In June 1993 Ali al-Nasri, rapporteur of the committee, announced that it had visited Juba and that its report would be submitted to the government by the end of the month. He said that "the committee [had] found no evidence of improper action by the military courts or the army". In September 1994 the chairperson of the TNA's Human Rights Committee told Amnesty International that the report had been passed to the government but had not been made public.

The UN Special Rapporteur on Sudan has expressed grave concern about human rights violations in Juba and submitted a list of "disappeared" prisoners to the authorities in late 1993. In February 1994 the government commented that the commission of inquiry blamed the delay in the production of the report on the "continuous flow of lists" of prisoners, for which it appeared to hold the Special Rapporteur responsible.

The government criticized the Special Rapporteur for not referring "to the intense conflict which took place within and around the town, and [for choosing] to portray the conflict as reprisals undertaken by the government in cold blood". Reprisals in cold blood, however, exactly describe many of these "disappearances" and extrajudicial executions after summary trials. Many of the reported human rights violations took place days, if not weeks, after the SPLA had been repulsed.

'THE TEARS OF ORPHANS'

Camillo Odongi Loyuk, a former soldier working as a senior civil servant, was arrested in Khartoum on 1 August 1992. On 15 September Camillo Odongi Loyuk, handcuffed to the bars of a window, died in a "ghost house".

'Disappearances' in Khartoum

Not all of those arrested on suspicion of collaboration with the SPLA in Juba were arrested in the south. Southerners were also detained in Khartoum. Camillo Odongi Loyuk, a former soldier working as a senior civil servant, was arrested in Khartoum on 1 August 1992. He had arrived from Juba only a few days before, apparently to put his daughters into school. Security men took him to an unknown destination in Khartoum. On 12 September Camillo Odongi Loyuk was brought to a "ghost house" in Khartoum. He was handcuffed to the bars of a window. A cord with a sliding noose which tightened as he moved was bound round his testicles. He was beaten. Over the next few days he was denied food and water. He died on 15 September.

George Oketch, a lieutenant-colonel in the paramilitary forces attached to the Department of Wildlife, was arrested on 30 July 1992, in Khartoum. He has not been seen since although it is rumoured that he was taken back to Juba. Captains Abalang and Lako, also with the Department of Wildlife, were reportedly arrested in September. Their fate is not known.

CHAPTER 4

The treatment of captured SPLA soldiers

> "There was an SPLA soldier wounded in Muniki [a Juba suburb]. He went into a house where there was a woman. She told him to leave, she begged him. She had children. He said he would go after dark. She sent for a friend to get medical help. The friend went straight to the army. They surrounded the house. They called to her and she went to the door. They hit her, went into the house and dragged out the soldier. Then they shot him. The body was left there for two or three days before people dared to bury it."
>
> Eye-witness to the killing of an SPLA soldier in July 1992

There is almost no clear information about the fate of combatants captured in conflict zones. However, the war is notable for the lack of captured prisoners in detention. This appears to be because the government regularly executes captured combatants if they cannot be used for intelligence purposes. SPLA soldiers who give themselves up voluntarily to government forces appear to be at less risk of execution.

In June 1992 seven wounded SPLA soldiers captured in Juba were tortured in a building near military headquarters known as the "White House" before being shot. Their arms and legs were tied behind their backs and they were suspended from the ceiling. They were then left hanging for several hours. Hot chilli pepper was rubbed into their wounds and they received severe beatings.

Torture in southern Sudan

Prisoners detained by Military Intelligence officials, PDF or other security authorities in southern Sudan are at serious risk of torture. This is particularly true of captured SPLA combatants. The fullest reports of torture in the war zones have come from Juba, although torture is by no means confined to the city. In March 1993, 32 men from SPLA-held areas were reportedly arrested and tortured after they went to the government-controlled town of Aweil looking for food. Their testicles were cut off and their ears severed. Twenty-two reportedly died.

In Juba, the "White House", an army barracks near the White Nile bridge, known as the Mechanized Battalion, and the headquarters of the Internal Security agency have all become notorious as torture centres. A prisoner arrested in early 1992 for possession of

'THE TEARS OF ORPHANS'

anti-government leaflets has described being tortured in the "White House", and put into a room with 25 other men and women: "They all carried the signs of torture. One had burn marks all over his body. A hot iron had been pressed on his flesh."

Aware of the international publicity that had begun to focus on the "White House", by 1993 the authorities in Juba were no longer using it as a detention centre.

Although by late 1992 government forces had pushed the SPLA back many kilometres from Juba, there were still persistent reports of torture. In May 1993 a senior official from Kapoeta was arrested and tortured by PDF volunteers from northern Sudan after a gun was discharged near their barracks. In this instance army officials intervened to free the man.

There are persistent reports that Military Intelligence officials, soldiers and members of the PDF torture prisoners arrested in the Nuba mountains. In addition to beatings, torture methods that have been used in the Nuba mountains include tying a bag containing chilli powder over the prisoner's head. A former prisoner has described a technique called "the plane takes off":

"The prisoner's elbows are tied to his knees and a wooden pole is pushed through the gap. He is left hanging for days. They give him drops of water and keep flogging him."

Prisoners who are reported to have died under torture include Mohamed Hamad and Ramadan Jaksa, both from Dilling. Khalifa Naway, a 51-year-old miner, and Shaib Sabreya, a 27-year-old farmer from al-Maryam, were tortured reportedly by troops in the Tima area who then accused them of being members of the SPLA. In April 1992 Ismael Sultan and Sheikh Hamdin, a chief from Katla south of Dilling, were reportedly tortured to death in al-Obeid. Ahmad Nasser was reportedly arrested in Dilling in May 1992, deliberately blinded and then released.

> "When a perfumer blends one kind of rose-water with another, he develops a fragrance which pervades the whole town."

Khalid al-Mubarak from the play
Ostrich Feathers
Reproduced with permission of the author

*Would you please stop pestering me
so that you and I
do not have to start questioning
each other's racial origin
so that you and I
can live together in peace
in this Sudan.*

*Would you please note
this Sudan you claim to be Arab
in the heart of Africa
has always been me
and only me.
Sudan is me!*

*Yet I do not want to remind you
of your Arab root
because
you're a human being like me,
with equal rights to live
in this land of the Blacks —
This Sudan!*

Sirr Anai Kelueljang, *This Sudan!*
Reproduced with permission of the author and New Beacon Books Ltd. (London)

5

Exploiting ethnicity

Both the government and the SPLA have exploited ethnic differences and competition over resources in ways which have pitted community against community and resulted in the massive abuse of human rights. While this has been a feature of the war throughout southern Sudan, this chapter focuses on two specific geographical areas, the area around northern Bahr al-Ghazal, inhabited mainly by Dinka and Luo, and the Nuba mountains of South Kordofan.

The hidden war in northern Bahr al-Ghazal

Since 1992 a largely unreported war has been fought in northern Bahr al-Ghazal. Troops and the PDF forces have used scorched-earth tactics to clear civilians from the strategically important railway line that links north and south Sudan and which the government uses to transport troops, military supplies and food to its garrisons. Troops and PDF have been responsible for scores of extrajudicial executions, for the use of civilians as hostages, for rape, for the abduction of women and children, for the destruction of villages and the pillaging of livestock. There are many reports alleging that abducted women and children are taken into domestic slavery in western Sudan. Both government forces and SPLA soldiers have looted UN relief trains which also use the line.

For the Dinka and Luo civilians, the railway line is both a salvation and a threat; in the mid- to late 1980s, tens of thousands of civilians fled along the line to escape famine and the ravages of *murahaleen*. In 1992 government forces opened the railway line for trains carrying arms and food. In mid-1993 the World Food Program (WFP) began using the line to

'THE TEARS OF ORPHANS'

Dinka villages and cattle camps in northern Bahr al-Ghazal have been raided by PDF militia clearing people away from the railway link between north and south Sudan. Since 1992 hundreds of people have been killed and thousands of head of cattle stolen. © *David Stewart-Smith/Katz*

transport relief food to Wau and Aweil, the major government-controlled towns in northern Bahr al-Ghazal, and to rural areas controlled by SPLA-Mainstream.

While WFP trains travel without military escort, government trains are heavily armed. Each is escorted by soldiers walking ahead and beside the train and by mounted PDF forces. They are deployed to clear civilians and SPLA from a wide swathe of territory on each side of the railway line. This has involved the indiscriminate killing of civilians, the abduction of women and children, the looting of property and livestock and the destruction of standing crops and homesteads.

The area is racked by famine, caused both by the war and several years of alternating drought and flooding. The UN Operation Lifeline Sudan (OLS) air-drops food at several centres away from the line and a number of non-governmental organizations run feeding centres. This aid is, however, only a proportion of what is required. Malnourished and desperate civilians face impossible choices: to stay near the line in the hope of food from passing trains but at risk of being killed by the PDF or to move away from the line to try and secure meagre food rations in the lands of others.

CHAPTER 5

The SPLA claims to give civilians information about which train is a UN food train and which is a government train. This information has not always been correct and villagers from south of Aweil, interviewed by Amnesty International in June 1994, expressed distrust of the SPLA; the SPLA has itself looted unescorted food trains.

When government forces opened the railway line in 1992 there was heavy fighting between government and SPLA in the north of Aweil. PDF units were dispatched to raid Dinka cattle camps and villages. Government officials reported that around 85,000 people were displaced. Dinka alleged that the PDF troops had abducted 46 boys and 150 young women, "whom they divided among themselves as their wives". At least 30 children were reportedly kidnapped by militia men lying in wait along the railway line as people trekked north.

This was a foretaste of a now familiar pattern. In February and March 1993 another train, which the government said was carrying food, came south, escorted by around 3,000 PDF and government troops. Along the line PDF and government soldiers were responsible for extrajudicial executions, rapes and abductions, with yet more human rights violations occurring as the train returned north in April. The PDF reportedly killed civilians between Malual and Aweil town and raped scores of displaced women at Meiram. As the train returned north the PDF was reported to have captured and extrajudicially executed Luo villagers from Akongdair and Pankuel. More than 300 women and children were abducted at various places along the way. Southern Sudanese government officials in Aweil apparently succeeded in freeing many of the captives. However, no action appears to have been taken against PDF members responsible for killings, rape or abduction.

Another military train passed along the line in June and July 1993. As the train moved south PDF troops fanned out, killing adults, abducting children, destroying standing crops and looting cattle. An eye-witness has described extrajudicial executions at Panjap station, south of Aweil.

"The horsemen [PDF] made us dance. We went to the station and they gave us groundnuts and made us dance. Then they told us to go away. We walked a short distance and they came at us from behind, from the train. They shot at us — we ran into the grass. Garang Akol, he was a young man, was killed. So were Acuor and Geng Can."

'THE TEARS OF ORPHANS'

Five elderly men were reported to have been extrajudicially executed at Kanji station, approximately 65 kilometres further down the line.

In February 1994 the UN Special Rapporteur on Sudan reported that the train was carrying 217 abducted children by the time it arrived in Wau. They were held for 17 days in Wau railway station; the authorities still did little to intervene while the train and the PDF were in Wau. The train then returned northwards. In Aweil the local authorities apparently intervened and freed around 150 children but took no further action against the PDF. When the train reached the Korrok area a further 19 children were captured. Around 80 are reportedly still missing.

In January 1994 another military train passed along the line, meeting stiff resistance from the SPLA south of Malual, with casualties on both sides. There were also reports of serious human rights violations. At Wedweil government troops reportedly captured three men and amputated their right hands. At Magai, 25 kilometres east of Kanji station, seven people are reported to have been extrajudicially executed and the village burned down by PDF troops. Some 30,000 people were displaced.

In May 1994 a UN food train left western Sudan. This train was looted by both government and SPLA soldiers and arrived empty in Aweil. A tragic sequence of events then unfolded. Luo civilians south of Aweil, unaware that the UN train had been emptied and was still in Aweil, came to the railway and encountered a heavily escorted military train proceeding southwards. There were killings and abductions in each station in territory not under government control and thousands of civilians were displaced from their homes by PDF outriders.

A man from the Akongdair area 25 kilometres east of the line described events at Panjap station, after people had been surrounded by PDF forces:

> "Then one of them said 'shoot them'. Everyone ran and shooting started. Akol Lual, he was killed. He was married with a small child. There are others who were taken and are missing. Akol Bol, she is missing. I don't know what has happened to her."

Some 50 people reportedly died at Mondit, the next station in an area not under government control, and several men and women were abducted and made to accompany the train southwards,

CHAPTER 5

Dinak prepare to sacrifice a bull in a religious ceremony at a traditional shrine.

evidently as hostages to prevent SPLA attack. Men and women were divided into separate groups. A number of women were reportedly raped; both men and women were hit by soldiers demanding information on SPLA in the area. The people were then told to run and the troops opened fire. The surrounding countryside was raided for three days by PDF forces.

Deng Dut, an elderly man from Bahr Mayen, described being taken with the train as it continued south:

"The soldiers lined us up and began to say 'Where is the SPLA?' We did not know. They beat people. I could not run, I was too weak. I fell over. The soldiers shot at people as they ran. I saw the soldiers kill two people they had wounded. Makuei Geng was hit by a stick on the head. Madut Maan was hit with an axe. Other wounded people managed to drag themselves away and are getting treatment in clinics in the villages."

Similar incidents took place at Gana and at Kanji further down the track. Some 30 civilians were shot and killed by government troops.

The persistent and gross violation of human rights along the railway line is a vivid example of the deliberate targeting of the

'THE TEARS OF ORPHANS'

civilian population by government military forces. The authorities have taken no action against those responsible for extrajudicial executions, rape and other human rights violations.

The government has not denied that soldiers and PDF forces are responsible for gross human rights violations. In November 1993 the government responded to the interim report of the UN Special Rapporteur on Sudan by claiming that the trains passing down the line are heavily defended because the authorities are committed to defending relief supplies from attack by the SPLA. The response accuses the Special Rapporteur of implicitly suggesting that "the Government [should] leave the civilian population to die of hunger rather than fight the rebels who block the food supplies". While the government does have the right to defend its trains, this can in no way be understood to include military tactics which involve the deliberate murder and ill-treatment of civilians, as it is doing in northern Bahr al-Ghazal.

The recurring pattern of gross violations along the railway line also raises questions about the UN's relief operation in Sudan. These questions relate to the monitoring and enforcing of security guarantees by both government and SPLA and the importance of ensuring that local people are fully informed about which trains are carrying food for public distribution. The use of the railway line to deliver food aid has complicated an already difficult situation for the civilian population in the area. The UN cannot be held responsible for the behaviour of either the government or the SPLA; but it is clear that in June 1994 at least the guarantees of safe passage negotiated by the UN failed to secure the safety of the civilian population and the flow of information to the civilian population was inadequate.

The fate of women and children abducted in northern Bahr al-Ghazal

There are persistent reports that women and children have been captured and detained by the PDF in Bahr al-Ghazal. As with children abducted by the PDF in the Nuba mountains these people, whose detention is arbitrary and apparently results from their ethnic origin, are reportedly taken into domestic slavery in Darfur and Kordofan.

The taking of slaves was a well-established practice in 19th-century Sudan but was virtually eradicated in the 20th century. However, the government policy of arming local communities to prey on their neighbours has revived the slave trade. PDF forces from western Sudan appear to regard captured children as legitimate war booty. The testimony of children who have escaped describes enforced agricultural and domestic labour, renaming of children and enforced conversion to Islam. Abducted women and adolescent girls are at risk of rape; many are reported to have been taken as concubines.

The government strongly denies allegations that the abduction of women and children, or their subsequent abuse, has official sanction. There are also provisions within the penal code prohibiting abduction, kidnapping and forced labour. Local officials in northern Bahr al-Ghazal have freed children taken by PDF troops. However, it appears that once children are removed from southern Sudan or the Nuba mountains their chances of being freed through official intervention are seriously reduced.

Relatives who make efforts to locate their children have to do so on their own, a difficult and potentially hazardous enterprise because the slave-holders regard them as the enemy in the context of the civil war. If, as sometimes happens, the children are found, relatives may try and buy the child's freedom. Some relatives have taken slave-holders to court and in some cases have had their children returned.

In August 1993 the government responded to concerns raised by the UN Committee on the Rights of the Child by simply denying that slavery existed:

"[S]ituations which are completely different from slavery have been wrongly depicted as enslavement. In reality, however, they involve tribal disputes and arguments over pasture and water resources in some areas where there is an overlap between tribes. As a result each tribe involved in a dispute captures members of the other tribe or tribes while waiting for the conflict to be settled according to tribal conditions and customs."[10]

Ultimately, debating whether the practice of abducting women and children and their servitude in domestic captivity constitutes slavery or some other social practice is irrelevant. The government's response to the Committee on the Rights of the Child acknowledges that people are abducted; the abductors are members of the armed forces and PDF militia, also a government force. The issue, therefore, is what action the authorities have taken to keep their forces under control, to prevent the practice, and to remedy it when it takes place. The evidence indicates that the government is, at best, condoning the taking of women and children into arbitrary detention by people acting in the government's name.

Laying waste to the Nuba mountains

The Nuba of South Kordofan have a special place in Sudan's war. Their political identity is that of an African minority in what many Nuba see as an Arab-dominated society. Many Nuba claim that of all the peoples in Sudan who regard themselves as Africans they are the most exposed to the possible political and cultural domination of the Arab north.

The Nuba are a collection of ethnic groups speaking more than 50 related languages who share a common culture and identity. Economically they are settled subsistence farmers working land in the hill massifs that rise out of the flat plains of Southern Kordofan. Christianity and Islam are both well established among the Nuba.

For a decade the government has attacked the Nuba, using *murahaleen* and PDF forces raised from the Hawazma and Misseriya — ethnic groups who graze cattle on the plains between the mountains — to raid Nuba villages thought to be sympathetic to the SPLA and kill civilians with impunity. Regular government troops, meanwhile, have massacred villagers and arrested and killed educated Nuba.

Counter-insurgency military action has left thousands of Nuba civilians dead and tens of thousands displaced in so-called "peace villages" in areas under government control. Women have been raped; women and children abducted. The destruction of homes, grain stores, livestock and crops has created a famine in rural areas, deliberately exacerbated by military action to sever areas not under government control from the outside world. Food supplies and relief aid have been poured into government-held towns to entice people to leave SPLA-controlled zones. The government has prevented international non-governmental organizations and UN agencies from establishing relief programs in the area.

Hundreds of Nuba leaders and political activists, particularly former members of the mainly Nuba SNP, have been arrested. Scores have "disappeared", unaccounted for by the government. Most arrests have taken place in southern Kordofan, but Nuba have also been arrested in Khartoum and other northern cities.

CHAPTER 5

The Nuba of southern Sudan have suffered gross human rights violations during the civil war between government troops and the SPLA. Thousands have been killed and tens of thousands of others cleared from their villages by force and settled in government-controlled "peace villages".
© *Peter Moszynski*

The *jihad* against the Nuba

The tactic of direct assault on civilians intensified after the regional military authorities declared a *jihad* against the SPLA-Mainstream in January 1992. At the same time the government began establishing the "peace villages" where people displaced by conflict were forcibly resettled.

In January 1992 Omar Suleiman Adam, the Assistant Governor for Peace and Rehabilitation Affairs in Kordofan State, announced that the authorities had prepared 22 "peace villages" to absorb and resettle 90,000 "returnees" from the SPLA. The government defines a "returnee" as anyone who has left an SPLA-controlled area. Omar Suleiman Adam said the villages were part of a project designed to absorb 500,000 people. The government presented these plans as a development initiative for Southern Kordofan. The "peace villages" were mainly displaced persons' camps in Northern Kordofan, many kilometres from the home areas of the Nuba, or camps situated close to mechanized agricultural schemes around the fringes of the mountains. By September 1992 the government had revised the extent of the policy. Omar Suleiman Adam announced

79

that the project would now absorb only 143,000 "returnees", in 89 "peace villages".

In 1992 the western mountains between Lagowa and Dilling, home to the Kamda, Tuleishi, Katla and Tabaq sections of the Nuba, bore the brunt of government military action. For example, in February 1992 PDF troops killed 25 villagers in the al-Faus area. In March and April more than 40 civilians were massacred around Jebel Tabaq.

The government and the SPLA agreed a cease-fire in June 1992, but deliberate and arbitrary killings by the army and PDF in al-Faus continued. In June 11 civilians were killed in al-Faus and in July a PDF unit attacked the village of Oma and killed five men and a woman.

A former security official from Kordofan who witnessed assaults on Nuba villages in the Tuleishi area in July and August 1992 described the government's tactics. He said the attacks began with tanks surrounding the target area and shelling the hills to eliminate possible SPLA opposition:

"Then ground troops entered the villages, shooting indiscriminately and killing hundreds of civilians. Young men, if they were still in the villages, were often executed on the spot. The people left behind, mostly women, children and the elderly, were gathered and trucked away to Kadugli...The purpose of the military is to evacuate the whole area because they are afraid that the villagers will join the SPLA.

"Many women were raped by the soldiers. During the shelling most houses caught fire. Houses which had not been destroyed were set alight later. Cattle were taken to Kadugli.

"The people were loaded on to trucks each of which could transport about 80 persons. Many had to walk to Kadugli under army guard. The dead bodies were left behind as prey for the animals. Only when there was time were corpses buried in mass graves dug by bulldozers."

This former security official had access to military radio reports which, he claims, indicated that between 50 and 60 Nuba villages were destroyed in this way between May 1992 and March 1993.

There are reports of rape of women held by the military. A

CHAPTER 5

woman from the Moro Hills who went to Kadugli in October 1992 was raped by soldiers in Kadugli barracks:

> "When I arrived I discovered that people were herded together like cattle. I left to go back [home]. But on the way I was taken by soldiers and tied down. I was...taken to the barracks. I refused them...Once I was tied they did a lot of things to me."

By November 1992 there was no trace of a cease-fire. Hundreds of villagers were reportedly killed in assaults on villages in the western and southern hills in late 1992 and early 1993. In December 1992 villages around Tima were attacked by a combined PDF and army force from Lagowa, 35 kilometres to the south. Scores of unarmed civilians are reported to have been extrajudicially executed at al-Maryam. The forces then moved on to attack villages to the west and north. Thirty-three women and children were reportedly abducted from Wali by the militia.

In December 1992 and January 1993 a series of Nuba villages in the Heiban and Moro areas were attacked by PDF and government soldiers. More than 100 civilians are reported to have died around Tumbira in December. Survivors report that the village was attacked in the middle of the night, and that people were burned to death in their homes or shot as they fled. Nine people were extrajudicially executed during a PDF raid on al-Lubi in the Moro Hills. In late 1992 the PDF attacked Karkari al-Beira, a village some 50 kilometres east of Kadugli. Many houses were burned down, but the people returned and rebuilt the village only for it to be attacked again on 13 January 1993. This time scores of people were reportedly killed and 400 homesteads and the church were destroyed.

In December 1992 a peace agreement between the Awlad Omran clan of the Misseriya Humr and the SPLA opened up pastures around lake Abyad to Awlad Omran cattle, and trade between the SPLA-held areas of the Nuba mountains and other parts of western Sudan. In February 1993 an Awlad Omran caravan was captured by government forces at Hafir al-Dibeikir between Muglad and Buram. About 70 traders were taken prisoner and accused of collaborating with the SPLA. They were transferred to al-Obeid prison where they remained as of July 1993 without charge or trial. Amnesty International has not been able to establish whether they have been released.

In January 1994 there was further military action. In the Shatt

'THE TEARS OF ORPHANS'

Kamal Tutu, a Nuba from the village of al-Atmur al-Nagrah was tied up by Sudan government forces and thrown into a burning church in December 1992. © *Peekaboo*

area, Mahmud Issa was reportedly killed by a PDF member as he tried to defend his wife from rape. There are reports that PDF troops ambushed and killed more than 60 civilians travelling from Lagowa to Dilling. Also in January, a group of Nuba travelling from Kadugli to Dilling were captured by the PDF at Kurgal. Seventeen were shot dead, among them Salah Ibrahim and Hussein Abdalla. A number of survivors are reported to have been severely beaten by security officials during interrogation.

Destroying the Nuba leadership

The other dimension of the government's war in the Nuba mountains has been the targeting of Nuba leaders suspected of opposing the government. Educated Nuba, former SNP members, traditional leaders in areas thought to be sympathetic to the SPLA, civil servants, health workers, school teachers and others have been detained without charge or trial and tortured. Others have "disappeared" and many have been extrajudicially executed.

A pattern of arrests, killings and "disappearances" became apparent in late 1990 and intensified in 1991. In July 1991 Hamdan Hassan Koury, a lawyer from al-Lagori living in Kadugli, was detained for one month. Immediately after his release, he was rearrested with his father. Both men were reportedly taken outside the town and shot. Others arrested in 1991 who have not been seen since include al-Sir Abdel Nabi Malik, an employee of the Soil Survey Department; Kamal Kano Kafi, a radio technician, and Ibrahim Marmatoun, an employee of the Water Department. The authorities have failed to account for these men.

A chief from Jebel Otoro, west of Heiban, was the sole survivor of a massacre of scores of chiefs in late 1991.

> "We were called for a chiefs' meeting by the government, but when we went there we found there was no meeting. We were all arrested, detained and had our hands tied behind our backs. We spent 59 days in prison. We were 68 in the prison, all of us from the Nuba mountains. One night, around 9pm, we were taken out [of] the prison. We were put on a truck [and driven into the countryside]. They shot us. I was shot in the back of the head. The bullet went through here and smashed my jaw. I fell unconscious...all the others died but I survived."

Scores of Nuba men have been detained without charge or trial

'THE TEARS OF ORPHANS'

for periods lasting from a few weeks to several years on suspicion of being government opponents. Abu Bakr Hamad, a religious teacher from Dilling reportedly arrested in February 1990, reportedly remained in al-Obeid prison in September 1992. It is not known if he has been released. More recent detentions include the arrests in May 1992 of al-Khair Hussein Walkiz, the clerk of Dilling Court, and Mahmud Hamid, secretary to the district commissioner, with five other men in Dilling. In July 1992 a further six men, among them the administrator of a mosque, were arrested in Dilling. All these people were transferred to al-Obeid prison. Mahmud Hamid is known to have been held for one month and was reportedly tortured. In August 1992 Adil Hassan Khair al-Sid, a postal worker, and six others were detained in Kadugli, reportedly after SPLA troops made a limited incursion into the town.

Ismail Gibril, an Anglican priest, was arrested in September 1992 in Dilling on suspicion of complicity with the SPLA. He was released in October but rearrested in November. He was released early in 1993.

In May 1993 Hamid Yacoub, a Nuba working overseas, was arrested as he returned from Kadugli to Khartoum. Military Intelligence officials stopped the bus on which he was travelling in a remote area 75 kilometres north of Kadugli town. Hamid Yacoub was taken into the bush, accused of helping the SPLA, blindfolded and threatened with execution. He denied involvement with the SPLA and was taken to Kadugli barracks. He was released after two weeks in incommunicado detention.

Also in May 1993, five men held in al-Obeid prison were reported to have been taken to Salara near Dilling where they were extrajudicially executed. The dead men, who were all from the Tuleishi area, included the chiefs Ahmad al-Zairiq Larfuk, Bashir Kano and Mekki Taisir Quli.

Nuba living in other parts of Sudan have also come under suspicion of being involved in political activity against the state. In June 1993 Mohamed Hamad Kowa, once an SNP leader, and Khamis Farajallah Kortel, a Christian priest, were arrested with three other leading members of the Nuba community in Khartoum. They were detained incommunicado without charge or trial for a few months. In October 1993 Guma Abdel Gadir, former Secretary General of Sudan's Post and Telecommunications Trade Union, was detained and held for several months without charge or trial.

*Sweep the house, daughter of chatter.
There's nothing to eat here.
Sweep the house, daughter of chatter.
There's nothing to eat here.*

*Nothing to eat, child of rope.
The ants probe; the mice have nothing.*

Eat Nothing sung by Nyapal Kong, translated into English by Terese Svoboda
Reproduced with permission of Terese Svoboda

6

The 'New Sudan': human rights abuses by the SPLA

The two SPLA factions control most of rural southern Sudan. Although some areas are more strongly held than others, in practice the SPLA factions have political authority over much of the south and parts of the Nuba mountains.

The SPLA claims to be building the "New Sudan". However, since its inception in 1983 the SPLA's approach to human rights issues has been characterized by ruthlessness, a lack of accountability and a complete disregard for the principles of humanitarian law. Deliberate attacks by each faction have been as responsible as government assaults for the destruction of rural communities. Prominent internal dissidents have been detained and some have been deliberately killed. Prisoners have been tortured, in some cases to death. Prison conditions in SPLA jails have been harsh to the extent of cruelty. Military discipline is only loosely maintained and internal disciplinary systems are applied arbitrarily on the whim of local commanders.

SPLA abuses in the Nuba mountains

The SPLA has been responsible for human rights abuses in the Nuba mountains. In particular, people suspected of being government informers and local leaders thought to be hostile to the SPLA have been deliberately and arbitrarily killed.[11]

Most SPLA abuses against the Nuba were reported in the early years of the war when the SPLA was establishing itself and consolidating its forces in the area. An SPLA unit on the fringe of the Nuba mountains in 1985 is alleged to have attacked Misseriya villages around Qardud and to have killed 100 villagers. In October 1987 the chiefs of the Nuba communities around Tira Lumum and Delami were

'THE TEARS OF ORPHANS'

Arapi, north of Nimule in southern Sudan. SPLA soldiers load an anti-aircraft gun. Government bombing of the area in 1994 led to a massive displacement of civilians. © *Crispin Huges/Panos*

CHAPTER 6

reportedly killed. SPLA killings were also reported in the Tuleishi area south of Dilling from April 1989. On 13 November 1989, six villagers were reportedly killed by SPLA forces which attacked al-Melaha.

More recently SPLA-Mainstream has responded to the government's attempts to clear people from the mountains by preventing villagers in areas under its control leaving for government-held areas, from where they are likely to be transferred to "peace villages". In January 1993 the SPLA imposed a civilian exclusion zone around Heiban. A village administrator named Abderahman from Abol, a few kilometres from Heiban town, was caught in the zone, summarily tried and promptly executed in public.

The split in the SPLA

In August 1991 SPLA commanders in Upper Nile, led by Dr Riek Machar Teny-Dhurgon and Dr Lam Akol Ajawin, split from the main body of the SPLA to form SPLA-Nasir and called for the overthrow of Dr John Garang de Mabior, whom they accused of being a dictator.

Warfare between the different factions of the SPLA broke out almost immediately and since then both factions, increasingly divided along ethnic lines (the Nasir faction being dominated by members of the Nuer ethnic group, Mainstream by the Dinka ethnic group), have been responsible for gross abuses of human rights. Each shares responsibility with the government for the creation of famine and a population dependent on international food relief. Each has deliberately assaulted villages and deliberately and arbitrarily killed thousands of civilians. Each faction has exploited ethnicity and in Upper Nile, in particular, ethnic difference has become a reason for killing.

The effect has been to devastate large parts of Upper Nile and parts of Eastern Equatoria, creating near-total dependency on food relief for hundreds of thousands of people. The civilian cost in lives and communities destroyed underlines the direct relationship between the abuse of human rights and the creation of a humanitarian disaster.

Killings by both factions in Upper Nile

Despite citing human rights abuses within the SPLA as one of the reasons for the split, within weeks of regrouping SPLA-Nasir forces

'THE TEARS OF ORPHANS'

Parajok, south of Torit in southern Sudan. Akuot Ngor fled with 42,000 others from the displaced people's camp at Atepi after government air raids and an attack apparently by SPLA-United. "We fled in panic with no chance to bring food. I have only this one dress which has become dirty from sleeping on the ground. The journey took 11 days and was very hard; I am old so I was pushed on a bicycle by my family. My daughter-in-law miscarried on the way and five of my family have still not arrived. We cannot stay here, there is no food or shelter and it is terribly cold at night." © Crispin Hughes/Panos

CHAPTER 6

had massacred Dinka and Mundari civilians in parts of Upper Nile controlled by SPLA-Mainstream.

The area hardest hit by the war between the SPLA factions has been the densely populated Duk ridge in Upper Nile. In October and November 1991 SPLA-Nasir forces raided lands controlled by SPLA-Mainstream and occupied by Dinka and Mundari civilians. They moved from homestead to homestead, killing civilians and looting property, food and animals. Hundreds of civilians were killed during the offensive. There were also reports that men had been castrated or disembowelled, that many women were raped and that women and children were abducted. Tens of thousands of cattle, the mainstay of the local economy, were stolen.

As SPLA-Nasir forces withdrew with looted cattle and foods, SPLA-Mainstream forces followed them. Captured Nasir soldiers were summarily executed. For example, 19 young Nuer men were reportedly tied up in a cattle byre near Bor and then speared to death.

The true casualty figures may never be known but it is estimated that as many as 2,000 people died. Approximately 200,000

In May 1993 SPLA-Mainstream troops attacked the village of Pagau, about 12 kilometres from Ayod; 32 women were lined up and shot. © Rory Nugent

'THE TEARS OF ORPHANS'

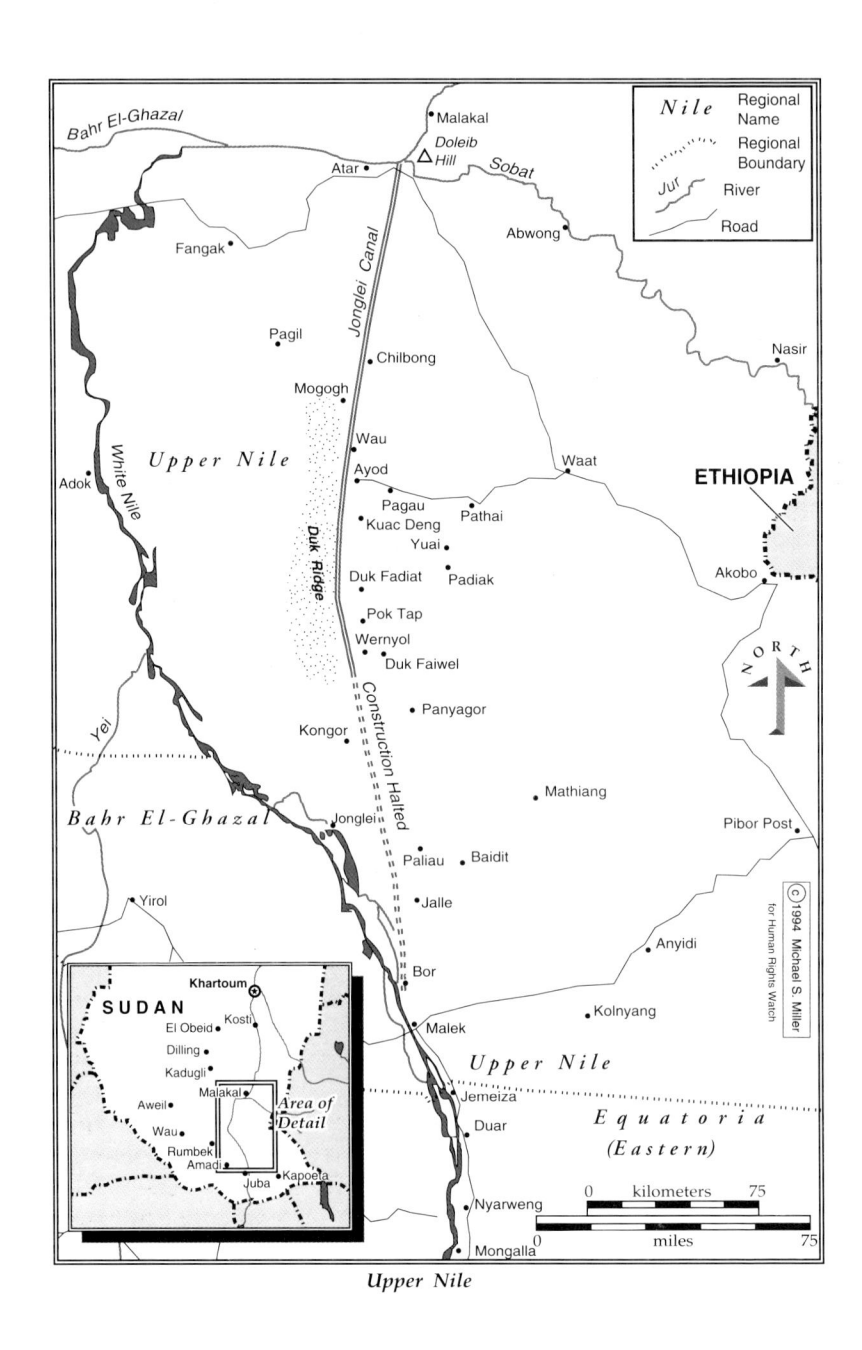

Upper Nile

CHAPTER 6

people were displaced by the attacks, which cut a swathe through one of the most densely populated parts of southern Upper Nile.

The factional war spilled over into other areas. In early 1992 SPLA-Nasir Nuer troops raided Dinka villages in Bahr al-Ghazal. Ninety-two defenceless civilians were reportedly killed, and at least 20 women and children were abducted. The raiders moved on to Wun Riit, a large Dinka cattle camp on the road to the Nile port of Shambe; there 40 civilians were reportedly massacred and several thousand cattle stolen.

SPLA-Mainstream forces in Upper Nile responded to the raids by attacking Nuer villages. In February 1992 SPLA-Mainstream troops attacked the village of Pagau, about 12 kilometres from Ayod; 33 people, including two children, were burned to death.

In mid-1992 SPLA-Nasir forces again raided Dinka communities along the Dinka/Nuer border. Poktap, a village 35 kilometres northwest of Kongor, was attacked and the families of two chiefs were killed. Further south at least 11 people, including seven women, were deliberately and arbitrarily killed in the village of Wernyol.

In September 1992 John Garang de Mabior's deputy, William Nyuon Bany, left SPLA-Mainstream and created the Unity group. This sparked further factional fighting in Eastern Equatoria. The Unity group received support from Nuer serving in Equatoria as well as troops drawn from a number of Equatorian ethnic groups, among them the Latuka, the Pari and the Didinga.

In March 1993 the SPLA-Nasir and Unity groups merged to form SPLA-United. The meeting to form the new group, in Kongor in Upper Nile, was attacked by SPLA-Mainstream. Four people are reported to have been executed after being captured by SPLA-Mainstream forces. Other civilians died in crossfire.

The retreating SPLA-United leadership was pursued northwards towards the Nuer town of Ayod, an important centre for food distribution and a focus for internally displaced people. Dinka civilians in the area claim that as SPLA-United troops retreated they abducted women and children and were responsible for killings in Duk Faiwil.

In April 1993 Ayod town was shelled by SPLA-Mainstream, which caused scores of civilian deaths. SPLA-Mainstream troops then entered the village and killed civilians indiscriminately. Tens of thousands of Nuer who had congregated at feeding centres in the Ayod region fled east towards the Sobat river. Over the next three weeks SPLA-Mainstream troops displaced thousands more Nuer

'THE TEARS OF ORPHANS'

civilians by moving through villages, killing anyone they found. The village of Pathai, 35 kilometres east of Ayod, was burned down and more than 100 civilians reportedly massacred. At the village of Pagau 32 women were lined up and shot. Eighteen children are reported to have been locked in a hut which was then torched. In Paiyoi, an area of dispersed settlement northeast of Ayod, 36 women were reportedly burned to death.[12]

Killings of civilians by SPLA-Mainstream in Eastern Equatoria

The defection of William Nyuon Bany in September 1992 led to a series of apparently ethnically motivated killings in Eastern Equatoria. SPLA-Mainstream forces pursuing William Nyuon Bany are reported to have killed defenceless civilians, including young children, from ethnic groups associated with the Unity group. A number of women were reportedly raped.

In early 1993 SPLA-Mainstream began systematically to destroy villages thought to be sympathetic to the Unity group. In January 17 Latuka villages around the Imatong and Dongotona mountain ranges were destroyed, displacing tens of thousands of people. Further north SPLA-Mainstream forces attacked Pari villages around the densely populated area of Jebel Lafon. Scores of civilians remain unaccounted for and are alleged to have been killed. Some 30,000 people were displaced and settled near farm plots deep in the bush. Between March and May 1993 SPLA-Mainstream forces looted and burned Didinga villages around Chukudum.

Fighting between SPLA-Mainstream and SPLA-United displaced hundreds of thousands of Dinka and Nuer civilians in Upper Nile between 1991 and 1993.
© *Rory Nugent*

CHAPTER 6

In late September 1992 SPLA-Mainstream soldiers also shot dead four foreign nationals. The victims were Myint Maung, a Burmese doctor who had worked in southern Sudan for many years, Tron Helge Hummelvoll, a Norwegian journalist, Vilma Gomez, a Filipino woman nurse, and Francis Ngure, a Kenyan driver. Both factions blamed each other, but subsequent investigations pointed to SPLA-Mainstream responsibility.

Human rights abuses after the split

In February 1992 SPLA-Mainstream released more than 40 long-term detainees, some of whom were prisoners of conscience. Some had been in custody since 1984. Several were senior commanders close to Dr John Garang de Mabior, before being suspected of disloyalty and arrested. They had experienced torture and harsh prison conditions in both Ethiopia, where they were imprisoned by the SPLA, and Sudan.

The split in the SPLA led to many new arrests and arbitrary killings within the factions' ranks, as each faction detained individuals suspected of being sympathetic to the other side. In many cases suspicion appears to have arisen solely on the basis of ethnicity.

Supporters of the Nasir group arrested several Dinka. The SPLA-Nasir leadership has said that they handed over 20 such prisoners to the International Committee of the Red Cross. However, Amnesty International has received information which suggests that others arrested were killed by SPLA-Nasir. Sixteen Dinka officers were reportedly arrested and later executed at Ketbek by SPLA-Nasir. Other officers killed included Captain Puol, a Dinka in charge of the airstrip at Nasir, who was summarily executed at Kut. In November 1991 another Dinka, Captain Michael Manyon Anyang, formerly a magistrate and an outspoken critic of the split, was arrested in Nasir and accused of attempting to blow up a compound used by the UN. He was summarily executed in mid-1992. SPLA-Nasir forces also killed 27 Nuba labourers at Baliet in early 1992, apparently because they were suspected of having had contact with SPLA-Mainstream forces.

SPLA-Mainstream has also been ruthless in dealing with soldiers suspected of disloyalty. Eight Nuer SPLA soldiers including Sergeants Wic Yual Tut and Michael Cuar Biel, suspected of trying to join the Nasir faction, were reportedly executed at Lasso in

'THE TEARS OF ORPHANS'

Eastern Equatoria in November 1991. In the same month, Captain Peter Reth Deng and First-Lieutenant John Jok Rambang were summarily executed in Yirol in Bahr al-Ghazal. In July 1992 six Nuer soldiers were executed at Ikotos in Eastern Equatoria.

After the defection of the Unity group in Eastern Equatoria in September 1992, SPLA-Mainstream launched an internal purge. Soldiers suspected of supporting the Unity group were arrested and in early November around 20 Acholi and Madi SPLA soldiers suspected of planning to defect were reportedly executed by SPLA-Mainstream at Nimule. Thirty Nuer soldiers were reportedly killed after they had been disarmed in Aswa. In December 1992 there were reports that over 200 deserters from SPLA-Mainstream forces stationed around Juba were disarmed and then deliberately killed near Tonj in Bahr al-Ghazal.

Not all soldiers suspected of disloyalty by SPLA-Mainstream were killed, or killed immediately. Some were arrested and held in custody; many were tortured or ill-treated. In September 1991 four SPLA soldiers, Paul Thong and William Maalia, both Nuer, and Manyang Kiir and Mayik Macar, both Dinka, were arrested in Pariang in Upper Nile and accused of supporting the Nasir group. They were taken to Limon in the Nuba mountains where Manyang Kiir was reportedly tortured to death. No evidence was found against the two Nuer prisoners, who were transferred to Kauda near Heiban. In early 1992, however, they escaped after getting word of a plot to assassinate them, because they were Nuer, in revenge for the killing of Dinka civilians in Bor by Nuer supporters of SPLA-Nasir.

The 1991 split in the SPLA provoked a political crisis in the movement's leadership in the Nuba mountains. Nuba soldiers unhappy with poor logistical support and the profile of Nuba in the movement made a series of demands on the SPLA-Mainstream leadership, which responded by ordering the arrest of the ring leaders. Awad al-Karim Kuku, Younis Abu Soder and 18 junior officers and other ranks were arrested in December 1991. They were held at Achuran in the Limon hills and severely beaten. In February 1992 the 20 Nuba and two Dinka held at Achuran were moved to Pariang. In June 1992 they were taken south to Karic, the SPLA-Mainstream command centre for southern Bahr al-Ghazal. Their treatment was harsh with repeated beatings; four men, Tariq Kodi, Abbas Mareq, Osman Rial and Mahmud Kodi, died on the way to

CHAPTER 6

Karic. In September 1992 the survivors were released and ordered to Kaya.

The arrest of suspected dissidents

Despite the releases in February 1992, a number of long-term SPLA detainees, among them Kerubino Kuanyin Bol, Arok Thon Arok, John Kulang Puot, Kawac Makuei Mayar and Martin Makur Aleu, remained in SPLA-Mainstream detention. At least six of those released were rearrested within a few days. After being held at several locations 13 prisoners were transferred to Morobo near Kaya on the west bank of the Nile. Before they reached Morobo, Thomas Kerou Tong, one of the SPLA's few pilots, was removed from detention and reportedly executed. In September 1992, five prisoners, among them Kerubino Kuanyin Bol and Arok Thon Arok, escaped. In the same month the remaining detainees were freed but ordered to remain in Kaya.

1993 began with further arrests, after SPLA-Mainstream claimed to have uncovered another plot against the leadership. Those arrested included nine prominent SPLA members who were taken into custody in Kaya and accused of masterminding the plot. They included

Martin Majier Gai, a judge and influential politician popular with the southern Bor Dinka, was arrested in 1993 after SPLA-Mainstream claimed to have uncovered another plot against the leadership. According to some sources he was deliberately executed in jail, though SPLA-Mainstream claim he was shot while trying to escape in 1993.

97

'THE TEARS OF ORPHANS'

Martin Majier Gai, a judge and influential politician popular with the southern Bor Dinka, Martin Kajivora and Martin Makur Aleu, all former long-term detainees. Others arrested included Younis Abu Soder and Awad al-Karim Kuku, previously arrested in 1991. On 14 January 1993, 19 officers from southern Bor were arrested and taken to a prison in Pageri where they too were accused of involvement in the coup plot.

In the following months some of the prisoners held in Pageri were reportedly tortured. Colonel Majur Nhial Makol has alleged that in February his foot was nailed to the floor. The chairman of a committee formed by SPLA-Mainstream to prepare the case against the prisoners found that they had been repeatedly beaten. Commander Makuei Deng Majuc sustained injuries to his head and back. Commander Bullen Alier Nhial received two broken ribs. Gabriel Mathiang Aluong's hearing was damaged. Major Robert Akuak Kudum died in March after being denied treatment for a medical condition exacerbated under torture. Captain Gabriel Majok Nyieth fell ill in March after being weakened by beatings and was also denied medical treatment until just before he died, in May 1993.

In April 1993 the committee's preliminary investigation concluded that there was no case against the men. This result displeased the SPLA leadership; the committee's chairman fled into exile and has reported that he was threatened by a senior SPLA officer. Some of the prisoners were released in September 1993, but most remained in custody until 26 January 1994.

The nine prisoners accused of leading the plot were executed according to some sources, although the SPLA-Mainstream leadership claims they were shot while trying to escape. SPLA-Mainstream persistently refused to account for the prisoners until June 1994 when it was announced that they had been shot trying to escape in 1993. The timing of this announcement is thought to relate to the declaration of a general amnesty "to all deserters and to those who have committed crimes against the Movement" by the first SPLA-Mainstream National Convention in April 1994 which would otherwise have made it necessary to produce the prisoners. In August 1994 Dr Carlo Madut Deng was reportedly abducted by SPLA-Mainstream from a refugee camp in northern Uganda, taken into custody and tortured in Nimule, southern Sudan.

There have also been arrests of dissidents in SPLA-United. In June 1994 John Luk, a senior member of SPLA-United, was arrested in Waat in Upper Nile on the suspicion that he was attempting to persuade the Gaatluak Nuer to desert Riek Machar Teny-Dhurgon and join Lam Akol Ajawin, expelled from SPLA-United in February 1994. In late June he was transferred to detention near Nasir.

Action against human rights abusers

The SPLA-Mainstream command is not known to have taken action against human rights abusers within its ranks, or to provide redress for the victims of abuses. It has remained silent on this issue.

SPLA-Nasir/United commanders have given contradictory responses, which suggests a failure to take adequate, and possibly any, action. In June 1994 Riak Machar Teny-Dhurgon told Amnesty International that the 1991 raids in Bor and Kongor had been the actions of a mob and it was difficult to identify the individuals responsible but that he had arrested Commander Simon Guarwic Dual. However, in 1992 he had told the UN that he had dismissed Commander Vincent Kuac Kuang, who, at the time of the Bor raids, was in charge in Ayod.

The consequences of the persistent failure to take action were again demonstrated in early 1994 when fighting erupted between different SPLA-United commanders, Gordon Kong Cuol and Gordon Kong Banypin. In April and May there was a series of battles between SPLA-United forces based around Waat, formed out of Lau Nuer, and forces based in Nasir and along the Sobat river, which were formed primarily out of Jikany Nuer. The fighting appears primarily to have been between the Lau and the Jikany Nuer over access to pasture. However, SPLA-United units joined in the attacks, allying themselves with communities on each side and leading assaults on Ulang, Nasir and other small centres along the Sobat river and south towards Akobo. Tens of thousands of civilians were displaced and an unknown number killed. Both commanders were arrested by the SPLA-United's leadership.

The administration of justice by the SPLA

Before the war judicial systems in the south operated according to customary law, administered by Chiefs' Courts, and the provisions of the Sudan penal code, administered by a system of District and High Courts run by legally qualified judges. Both factions of the SPLA have retained this system and the distinction between types of courts.

'THE TEARS OF ORPHANS'

SPLA-Mainstream soldiers at Kongor in Upper Nile help a wounded colleague to safety. SPLA-Mainstream and SPLA-United are fighting each other as well as the government. © Crispin Hughes/Panos

The SPLA has published its own legal code, introduced in 1983. This is a hybrid between a military code of discipline and a penal code for civilians. Since 1991 both factions of the SPLA have claimed to use this legal code. In addition, the provisions of the pre-1983 Sudan penal code are apparently invoked when they do not contradict the SPLA code.

The criminal justice system operating in SPLA-controlled areas fails to satisfy minimum international standards of fairness in almost every respect. The courts are not independent or impartial, it is not clear what law is applied, there is no right of appeal in death penalty cases and the right to seek pardon or commutation of a death sentence is rarely honoured in practice.

The SPLA legal code is theoretically administered through a three-tier system of courts-martial convened on an *ad hoc* basis. The highest court-martial acts as an appeal court for the two lower courts and as the trial court for capital offences. Personnel serving in the courts are appointed by local commanders, with the exception of the highest court which is appointed by the SPLA Chairman. Death sentences "ought to be" confirmed by the Chairman except when "communications with the headquarters are difficult because of enemy action or if morale or discipline dictate [when] a sentence of death may be confirmed by a Battalion Commander". When a sentence is being submitted for approval, a written copy of the investigation as well as a summary of the legal proceedings should be submitted to the confirming authority. This is an inadequate right of appeal as it contains significant clauses allowing the authorities not to uphold it. Additionally, in certain circumstances the death penalty can be carried out without approval.

There are no procedural guidelines for the SPLA legal code; there are no limits on the length of time a suspect can be held for investigation or any requirement for the accused to be brought to trial within a specified period. Investigations leading to prosecution in a court-martial are carried out by any officer on the orders of battalion deputy commanders. There are no guidelines governing systems of investigation.

The administration of justice through courts-martial has been arbitrary and chaotic within both factions of the SPLA. There is confusion between the status of the legal code as a system of internal military discipline in times of war and its role as a regulator of civilian conduct. The court system is characterized by an inadequate separation of powers between the executive and the judiciary; in a situation where the military is totally dominant it is easily abused. The legal code has been applied on the whim of local commanders. Court rulings have been ignored or overruled. Both SPLA-Mainstream and SPLA-United have been hampered by a shortage of legal personnel, with only 20 qualified judges between them. In June 1994 a former SPLA-Mainstream officer who was involved in the administration of justice told Amnesty International:

> *"The code is next to useless. You just have to use your experience. The system that has been created in the end relies upon principles which are more appropriate for customary law. These involve negotiating a settlement to a dispute. So if the aggrieved party is a senior official or if the demand for action comes from the leadership you know what you have to do...For those at the top, the regulation of justice is more to do with keeping balance between political forces. There is no real judicial system."*

In many cases the SPLA's legal processes have simply been

overruled or ignored. None of the political detainees arrested between 1984 and 1993 are known to have received a trial. Some cases were investigated — although most frequently investigations appear to have focused on extracting information rather than building a legal case.

Few, if any, death sentences are referred to the Chairman of SPLA-Mainstream, as required by the SPLA code. A local SPLA-Mainstream commander interviewed in June 1994 indicated that information about death sentences was often passed from his area, several hundred miles from SPLA-Mainstream headquarters in Eastern Equatoria, by radio. The practical realities of communications in war-torn Sudan, combined with the speed with which death sentences are carried out, makes it unlikely that written records of cases reach the Chairman.

The continued abuse of legal procedures within the SPLA to pursue short-term and often local political goals means that few soldiers in either faction view judicial systems with respect, creating a climate in which soldiers feel they can commit human rights abuses with impunity.

SPLA-United appears to have tried to address this problem in a limited way by holding some officers responsible for the actions of their troops. However, their sentences have not been commensurate with the severity of the crime. SPLA-Mainstream, in the context of human rights abuses at least, does not appear to have held officers responsible. The gap between the punishments and the severity of the crimes further undermines the judicial system and fosters impunity.

In April 1994 the first National Convention convened by SPLA-Mainstream passed a set of resolutions with the stated aim of establishing an independent judiciary, apparently to deal with civilian cases, and introduced new legislation. It resolved to establish a Law Review Committee to examine the suitability of new laws "and to propose amendments and changes where necessary". These developments appear to represent a recognition that previous legal provisions were inadequate. However, the key issue, yet to be tested, is whether new laws and their practical application will safeguard human rights.

*We will someday build it,
the homeland of our daily dreams:
...
Convert the prison into
a hospital
The banishment centre into
a college hall
The captives will become
a shift of working men
and women.
Instead of anguish and sorrow
there will resound a song
Instead of a deadly bullet
a sparrow will fly
hover above a fountain
and have fun
with kindergarten children.*

Sung by Mohamed Wordi, written by Mahjoub Sharif
Reproduced with permission of Mohamed Wordi

7

Responding to human rights criticism

Over the past five years the international community has repeatedly expressed its condemnation of the gross abuse of human rights by the Sudan Government and both factions of the SPLA. National and regional assemblies have held debates. The UN Commission on Human Rights and the UN General Assembly have passed resolutions. Special Rapporteurs and Special Envoys have been appointed. UN human rights theme mechanisms and the Committee of Experts of the International Labour Organisation (ILO) have issued comments. Non-governmental organizations working in the field of human rights have produced numerous reports. The Sudan Government has become increasingly diplomatically isolated.

The government is not insensitive to international pressure on human rights issues. In northern Sudan, the government's need to build popular support within Sudan while retaining a monopoly on power has combined with international pressure on human rights violations to cause it to introduce measures which are designed to disguise the true extent of repression. Some of these measures have had an impact on the pattern of human rights violations. Most detainees are not held for more than a few months now, although they may be rearrested shortly after release. The system of daily reporting to security offices immobilizes suspected political opponents without resort to formal detention. There have been periodic amnesties for political detainees and prisoners convicted of political offences. Perhaps the most important long-term measure is the creation of a compliant judiciary to implement legislation which ensures government control over all civil institutions.

In the war zones of southern Sudan the government has made no such efforts to cloak

'THE TEARS OF ORPHANS'

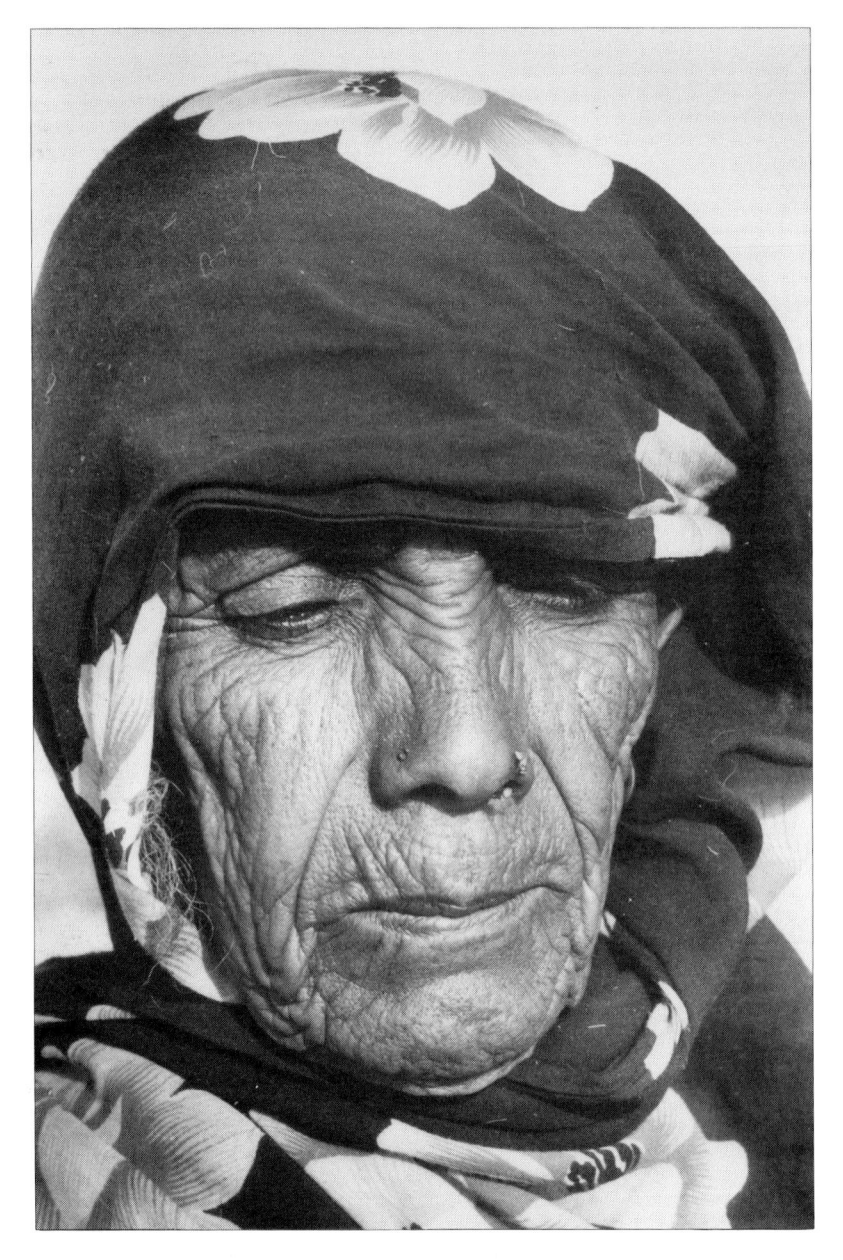

An elderly woman from Kordofan. © Panos

CHAPTER 7

repression in a veneer of legality. In fact, all parties to the conflict seem to believe they can abuse human rights with impunity. An important step towards improving the situation of human rights in the conflict zones would be to end the war through an agreement which contains human rights guarantees. International pressure and internal political considerations have resulted in negotiations about peace, but the talks have collapsed several times and progress on key political issues is slow.

While the world community, both governmental and non-governmental, has strongly condemned the human rights records of both the Sudan Government and both factions of the SPLA, this pressure appears to have reached an invisible diplomatic ceiling. The government and both factions of the SPLA have shown little sign that they are ready to make decisive progress towards human rights improvements. Among some governments, aware of the many resolutions that have been passed and the already considerable isolation of the Sudan Government, there is a sense of resignation, a sense that the international community is doing all it can with no results. Some governments have begun to play down the seriousness of the human rights situation in pursuit of their own political interests.

While many governments and non-governmental organizations have condemned continuing gross violations of human rights, the notion that the international community is doing all it can to exert pressure on the Sudan Government and both factions of the SPLA about human rights does not stand up to close examination. The appointment of a Special Rapporteur on human rights in Sudan by the UN in 1993 was an important and welcome step. However, neither his work and recommendations, nor the work of UN human rights theme mechanisms, have been backed by the resolutions passed by the UN and other international bodies. These resolutions have been forthright in their condemnation of the government and both factions of the SPLA but have made few practical demands for action. This is a serious failing.

Meanwhile, the government has adopted an aggressive approach towards its critics at the international level, by attempting to discredit intergovernmental bodies that expose human rights abuses in Sudan.

For the international community the issue of action in relation to the appalling situation of human rights violations in Sudan is a question of political will and vision. The work of the Special

Rapporteur needs adequate support. The international community should ensure he receives the fullest backing to fulfil his mandate.

Amnesty International is calling for the creation of an international monitoring body with the necessary level of resources and expertise to establish an on-the-ground monitoring presence in all parts of the country.

International human rights mechanisms and Sudan

Several UN bodies and human rights theme mechanisms have considered complaints against the Sudan Government. The UN Special Rapporteur on torture has sent numerous urgent appeals to the authorities, and in his 1994 report concluded that torture is systematic in Sudan. In a report issued in December 1993 the UN Special Rapporteur on extrajudicial, summary or arbitrary executions stated that he was "deeply concerned at the scale of the reported violations of the right to life in the Sudan, especially in the southern part of the country, both at the hands of the government security forces and of the different factions of the SPLA".[13] In a 1993 ruling which has implications for virtually every detainee arrested in Sudan, the UN Working Group on Arbitrary Detention found that 10 SCP members arrested in Khartoum in December 1992 were detained arbitrarily. The Working Group requested the government to remedy the situation of the 10 detainees. Eight had been released by early 1994.

The UN General Assembly has also publicly put human rights pressure on the government. In late 1992 international concern over human rights abuse in Sudan was intensified by the siege of Juba, in which hundreds of people had been extrajudicially executed or "disappeared". This sparked a debate at the UN General Assembly, which resolved to express deep concern at serious human rights violations and recommended that the situation be monitored.

In February 1993 the UN Commission on Human Rights resolved that the issue of human rights in Sudan should be put on the public agenda. A Special Rapporteur on the country, Hungarian lawyer Gaspar Biró, was appointed and issued an interim report which led the UN General Assembly, in late 1993, to express again its concern at continuing human rights violations. It also called on the Sudan Government to explain its obstruction of the efforts of the Special Rapporteur, especially with regard to retaliation against people who had contacted him.

CHAPTER 7

In 1994 the UN appealed for funding to enable them to provide 2.4 million war-affected people with food aid. © Sarah Errington/Panos

'THE TEARS OF ORPHANS'

The Special Rapporteur's full report, submitted to the Commission in February 1994, "firmly concludes that grave and widespread violations of human rights by government agents and officials, as well as abuses by members of the SPLA factions in zones controlled by them, continue to take place".[14] The report describes extrajudicial killings, summary executions, enforced or involuntary disappearances, systematic torture and widespread arbitrary arrests of government opponents. The Special Rapporteur also received reports of grave violations and abuses against women and children: "abduction, traffic, enslavement and rape carried out by persons acting as agents of the Government or affiliated with the Government".[15] The Commission resolved to extend the mandate of the Special Rapporteur for another year.

However, apart from the appointment of the Special Rapporteur, the Commission on Human Rights and the General Assembly have been long on rhetoric and short on action. At its 1994 session the Commission on Human Rights had only reached the stage of expressing "deep concern [at] reports of grave human rights violations", but had yet to come up with proposals for action, beyond calling for respect of international human rights instruments and humanitarian law, and urging the government to hold a judicial inquiry into the killings of four Sudanese employees of foreign relief organizations. The resolution even falls short of recommendations made by the Special Rapporteur, who had called for investigations into reported human rights violations in the Nuba mountains and into "reported cases of abduction of women and children, slavery, servitude, slave traffic, forced labour and other similar institutions and practices".[16]

The Organization of African Unity (OAU) has taken no effective action on the human rights crisis in Sudan. In October 1990 Amnesty International submitted a report documenting gross human rights violations in Sudan to the African Commission on Human and Peoples' Rights. The Commission declared the report admissible and asked the then Chairman of the OAU to request an in-depth study. He never replied. The Commission has repeatedly sought an invitation from the government to visit Sudan, but appears to have taken no further action. In 1994 the government indicated that it was agreeable to a visit in principle.

The international community appears to be focusing on the situation in the war zones and virtually ignoring the serious human rights situation in other parts of the country. The situation of human rights in the war zones is grave and merits decisive action, but the failure to address human rights abuses elsewhere in the country indicates complacency and fails to recognize the true dimension of the human rights problem in Sudan. The effect is to make respect for human rights a hostage to the peace process. While the end of the war is seen by many as a vital step in the creation of a secure future for the respect of human rights in all parts of Sudan, ending the war will not end human rights violations unless the government also ceases to arbitrarily detain, torture and kill its citizens at will.

A strategic response

In February 1994 the Sudan Government emphatically rejected the UN Special Rapporteur's report. The official response questioned the Special Rapporteur's competence, impartiality and personal motivation. The government has indicated that it will not cooperate with him. However, more significant than the attack on a person discharging the will of the international community was the government's attempt to characterize UN criticism of Sudan's human rights records as a response to the introduction of the 1991 Penal Code, an interpretation of *Shari'a* law, and therefore an attempt to manipulate "the noble issue of human rights [to] wage war on Islam".

This statement reflects one aspect of what appears to be the government's strategy to deal with pressure on human rights issues from the international community, particularly the UN. The strategy has apparently three elements: first, the government is attempting to portray criticism of human rights violations as anti-Islam; second, it is lobbying Arab and Muslim states and non-governmental organizations to establish international support; third, it has created a series of official structures to develop and communicate its message about human rights.

The clearest statement of the government's philosophy of human rights is laid out in *The Sudan document on human rights* which was adopted in July 1993 by the TNA — the government-appointed interim parliament — stressing, in particular, the place of human rights in the government's interpretation of Islam. It affirms Sudan's compliance with international human rights treaties. The document also attacks what it describes as the political exploitation of human rights by "states and voluntary organizations which have been governed by political considerations in their

'THE TEARS OF ORPHANS'

A crowd of 2,000 women demonstrated in Khartoum on 8 September 1993 protesting at United States policies towards Sudan. © *Associated Press*

overall conduct", a practice, the document claims, which has led to the destruction of national sovereignty and a "consequent loss of confidence in international law and institutions". Decisions and resolutions about the violation of human rights in Sudan are dismissed as contrary "to both truth and justice".

The document concludes with a charter, a statement of principles which is not legally binding. This forbids torture and ill-treatment and confirms that everyone has the right to be presumed innocent until proved guilty. However, some of its provisions define freedoms in ways that fall short of the human rights safeguards enshrined in international standards. For example, the charter declares that "human life is sacred and no one is permitted to attack it", but qualifies this with "other than as prescribed by law". Similar clauses qualify the declarations that "everyone has the right to [freedom of] thought, expression and worship and to practise the rites of their religion" and "no one may be arrested or detained or held in custody or expelled nor may his possessions be confiscated nor his liberty restricted". The law as it currently stands gives the Sudanese authorities sweeping powers of detention. Although the charter declares the right to a "full and fair trial", it fails to spell out the right of appeal. The document pays lip service to international standards while actually promoting principles which do not afford the same degree of protection.

In October 1992 the pro-government Sudanese Bar Association announced that it would hold an international conference on human rights in Islam which was eventually held in January 1993. The conference was an effort to win international support and discussed aspects of human rights in Islam. It voted to set up an organization called the International Islamic Organization for Human Rights which has since supported the government's human rights record.

Also in October 1992, the government announced the creation of a new committee in the Attorney General's office "to supervise human rights affairs". According to an official press release, the committee's brief was to "try to ensure that all state organs respect the laws preserving basic human rights and also to process complaints of human rights abuse and [to] try to redress any injustice". Later in the year the government claimed the committee had investigated violations of human rights and even brought criminal cases against perpetrators. However, there is no evidence that such investigations actually took place.

'THE TEARS OF ORPHANS'

In December 1992 the TNA created a human rights committee. This committee was said to be responsible for guaranteeing observance of human rights in accordance with the provisions of regional and international instruments signed by Sudan. One of the committee's first initiatives was the preparation of *The Sudan document on human rights*. In April 1993 government coordination of its response to criticism of its human rights record was strengthened by the creation of a "higher coordination council" for human rights chaired by the speaker of the TNA. In May 1993 Aldo Ajou Deng, chairman of the TNA's human rights committee, announced that it had investigated a large number of citizens' complaints and had found nothing "that could be regarded as a human rights violation within the recognized international framework". However, in January 1994 Aldo Ajou Deng fled into exile and denounced the human rights record of the government:

"Human rights violations have been in all aspects of life in Sudan. Racial and religious discrimination; indiscriminate killing of citizens in the south and Nuba mountains; unlawful arrest and 'disappearance' of opponents of the government; the kidnapping of young children for enslavement, religious orientation and military training have all become the unwritten law of the country."

Interviewed by Amnesty International, Aldo Ajou Deng said that the TNA's human rights committee had indeed tried to investigate allegations of human rights violation brought to it but its attempts were consistently blocked by the security services. In August 1994 his successor announced that the committee was investigating allegations of human rights violations.

Human rights are too important to be left to the political or military authorities within the government or the SPLA. The coming to power of the present government put an end to the development of an independent human rights community in Sudan. Activists have been detained or driven into exile. In southern Sudan, armed conflict and SPLA abuses have inhibited the activities of Sudanese seeking to promote human rights.

Initiatives by Sudanese networks and bodies to monitor human rights are vital if a human rights culture is ever to develop in Sudan. For those inside Sudan genuine human rights work can be dangerous; for those outside the country there is less danger but there are great difficulties in collecting and cross-checking information. The international community has an essential role in assisting Sudanese seeking to engage in human rights work.

Human rights and peace

The issue of human rights in Sudan extends well beyond the issue of the war. The government is responsible for the serious violations of human rights for reasons unconnected with the war in areas largely unaffected by it. However, ending the conflict is vital for the creation of a secure future for the respect of human rights in all parts of the country. A cessation in hostilities, especially through an agreement containing human rights guarantees and agreed mechanisms for the protection of human rights, might reduce the frequency of some of the most serious human rights abuses.

There has been little progress to date towards peace. An initiative mediated by the Nigerian Government on behalf of the OAU, involving all parties, began in May 1992 in the Nigerian capital, Abuja, but adjourned within a few days. A second round of talks between the government and SPLA-Mainstream was convened in Abuja in April 1993. A cease-fire was declared, but when the talks broke up in May SPLA-Mainstream announced that the cease-fire was over. Meanwhile SPLA-United was meeting a government delegation in Nairobi. In May 1993 the US Government attempted to mediate a cease-fire between the two SPLAs; both agreed to withdraw their troops from the so-called "hunger triangle" of Upper Nile, where they have been responsible for gross human rights abuses. Within a few weeks SPLA-Mainstream was responsible for attacks on civilian targets in the area supposedly devoid of troops.

In November 1993 the member countries of the Inter-Governmental Authority on Drought and Development (IGADD) — Kenya, Uganda, Eritrea and Ethiopia — launched a major peace initiative to address "the problem of southern Sudan". In January 1994 the IGADD foreign ministers met separately with the three parties in Nairobi; SPLA-United and SPLA-Mainstream agreed a cease-fire. Meanwhile the government launched a major offensive in Equatoria.

In March 1994 face-to-face negotiations took place and the parties committed themselves to a set of principles intended to facilitate the delivery of humanitarian relief. A further accord on access for relief supplies was signed in mid-May. Peace talks convened a few days later broke up with little progress. In July 1994

'THE TEARS OF ORPHANS'

The war has destroyed all basic services. Schools have been abandoned or burnt down. These children are being taught in a former agricultural centre near Kongor. Behind them are broken machines. © *Crispin Hughes/Panos*

CHAPTER 7

the parties met in Nairobi where the talks focused on two key areas: self-determination for the south and the relationship between the state and religion. The talks adjourned without agreement. A further round of talks collapsed in September, with no date set for resuming negotiations.

Whether or not the IGADD talks are reconvened and manage to resolve the serious political obstacles in the path of peace or not, any peace agreement needs to include the fullest human rights guarantees. International observers and mediators have a special role in helping ensure that this happens. In the meantime the importance of establishing respect for human rights is paramount.

A proposal for action

While the violation of human rights lies at the root of the conflict and the creation of the overwhelming humanitarian need in Sudan and must be addressed in any peace agreement, ultimately the prevention of human rights violations in Sudan is an issue with implications which go well beyond the peace process. Therefore it is important that human rights monitoring should not be seen as the same as cease-fire monitoring. There is an urgent need for the active monitoring of human rights in all parts of Sudan.

Those in authority, whether the government or either faction of the SPLA, need to demonstrate that they are fulfilling their obligations under the international human rights and humanitarian treaties to which Sudan is a party. The rhetoric of respect for human rights is no substitute for action.

Periodic visits by organizations not permanently based inside the country to research and advise on human rights issues should be encouraged. However, visiting delegations have only a limited capacity to carry out the sustained work required to help build respect for human rights in a country as vast as Sudan.

Amnesty International is calling for the creation by an appropriate intergovernmental organization of a team of international civilian human rights monitors to work with the authorities and the Sudanese public in all parts of Sudan to build respect for human rights. Amnesty International is calling on the Sudan Government and each faction of the SPLA to demonstrate their commitment to human rights by inviting such a monitoring team to establish itself in areas that they control and to provide the monitors with every cooperation.

'THE TEARS OF ORPHANS'

A Beni Amer girl from the Red Sea Hills, Sudan. © *Panos*

The role of the monitoring team should have two key aspects. The first should be the "active verification" of human rights violations. The monitoring team should be empowered to bring information to the attention of central and local authorities in the expectation of remedial action, and be able to follow up such cases until they are considered resolved. It should monitor appropriate disciplinary and other action taken by officials in relation to any offending personnel. In addition, the monitors should prepare public reports on their work, describing allegations of human rights violations received and recommendations made to the authorities to remedy either individual or systematic abuses of human rights.

Secondly, the monitoring body should work with Sudanese institutions to help build their capacity to ensure that respect for human rights is fully guaranteed. The monitors should encourage the authorities to establish effective systems of investigation and remedial action to combat human rights violations. They should work with the authorities to ensure the effective implementation of Sudan's commitments under the international human rights and humanitarian treaties that Sudan has ratified (see Appendix).

Monitors should be located in all 26 of Sudan's states, not just

CHAPTER 7

in major towns or cities. The full deployment of a human rights monitoring team would require the agreement of each of the three parties to the war. However, a partial or phased deployment would be possible with the agreement of only one party. The proposal extends beyond the war zones to include territory less affected by the war. It would therefore be possible for deployment to proceed in advance and independently of a cease-fire or peace agreement. This is true even of areas inside the war zone; large parts of the south are militarily quiet and there is already extensive deployment of international personnel in relief and development programs.

The international community has recognized the need and has accepted the burden of alleviating the disastrous humanitarian consequences of the war. Each year the OLS transports tens of thousands of tonnes of food, seed and medical supplies to areas controlled by the government and by both factions of the SPLA, while providing logistical support for scores of agencies engaged in relief and development work. It is time for the world community to complement this initiative by additionally investing in preventing the human rights violations that, in the final analysis, create the need for the international humanitarian intervention in the first place. A Sudan where human rights are respected will be a Sudan far less prone to humanitarian catastrophe.

There are many horizons that must be visited, fruit that must be plucked, books read, and white pages in the scrolls of life in which to inscribe vivid sentences in a bold hand...I hear a bird sing or a dog bark or the sound of an axe on wood - and I feel a sense of stability, I feel that I am important, that I am continuous and integral. No, I am not a stone thrown into the water but seed sown in a field.

Tayeb Salih from the novel *Season of Migration to the North*, translated by Denys Johnson-Davies
Reproduced with permission of the author and Heinemann Publishers (Oxford) Ltd.

8

Conclusions and recommendations

The problem of respect for human rights in Sudan extends well beyond the war zones. Arbitrary detention and torture continue as the government implements its political program, which involves dismantling the institutions of civil society. Even the inadequate safeguards for the rights of detainees are ignored by a security apparatus which acts as a law unto itself. The legal system contains penalties which are cruel, inhuman or degrading and as such are prohibited by international agreements. Specific action in respect of human rights has apparently more to do with image management than addressing fundamental issues.

In the war zones, far from the eyes of the world, the abuse of human rights is flagrant. The Nuba mountains are a closed area; entire communities are being systematically destroyed in a brutal counter-insurgency campaign. Government forces and SPLA soldiers have deliberately massacred civilians who have played no part in the conflict, solely on the basis of their ethnic identity or suspected political allegiance. Neither the government nor the SPLA appears to have taken any serious action to bring abusers to account.

A just and lasting peace with full human rights guarantees and mechanisms for monitoring compliance with these guarantees would be a step towards a future in which human rights are respected. However, as long as the government continues to arbitrarily detain opponents at will, to hold unfair trials, and to torture, Sudan will continue to witness human rights violations even if the war ends.

Governments adopt and are bound by international human rights and humanitarian law standards and bear a responsibility to ensure that these are respected at all times. Human rights abuses by the SPLA can never justify the abandonment of these fundamental principles. Neither should they be used as a means to divert attention from human rights violations by the government.

Human rights abuses by both factions of the SPLA are equally deplorable. Arbitrary killings by one faction do not justify reprisal killings by the other, let alone the targeting of entire social or ethnic groups on account of the actions of a few of their members. The fact that one side tortures and kills its prisoners of war is no excuse for the other to follow suit.

I. Recommendations to the government and both factions of the SPLA

1. Cooperate with the international community in promoting the deployment in all parts of Sudan of an international civilian monitoring body charged with monitoring human rights abuses

The **government** and each faction of the SPLA should cooperate with the monitoring body by:

- granting unimpeded and regular access to places of imprisonment and detention, to places where human rights violations are alleged to have been committed and to individuals seeking assistance or wishing to make complaints;
- permitting human rights monitors to conduct thorough and impartial investigations into allegations of torture, extrajudicial execution and deliberate and arbitrary killing;
- granting human rights monitors unimpeded access to local and national media.

Each party should:

- ensure that there are no reprisals against persons or organizations contacting the human rights monitoring body;
- act on the body's recommendations in respect of human rights.

2. Place human rights issues at the centre of any peace or cease-fire agreement

The signature of a peace accord would provide a particular opportunity to create a society based on respect for human rights. Any peace or cease-fire agreement should include a chapter specifying the rights and standards which both the **government** and the SPLAs

are to respect in both the transition and post-settlement periods. The chapter should include:
- rights defined in the Constitution and relevant national legislation (where these are in conformity with international standards);
- rights defined in international human rights instruments to which Sudan is a party and in other international human rights and criminal justice standards and principles.

The **government** and each faction of the SPLA should agree to account for past human rights violations and commit themselves to taking the following steps:
- ensure that complaints of human rights abuses are investigated by independent and impartial commissions of inquiry;
- suspend from their posts those being investigated for abuse, pending the outcome of the investigation;
- enforce the principle that those found guilty of human rights abuse should never again hold a post in which they have custody of prisoners or power to use or order the use of lethal force;
- publish lists of prisoners who have been arrested as a consequence of the conflict.

The **government** and each faction of the SPLA should authorize the UN to play a key role in the supervision of the human rights aspects of any peace or cease-fire agreements, in the investigation of alleged human rights abuses and in ensuring that corrective action is taken.

3. Order prompt and impartial investigations into all reported human rights violations

The **government** should publish the report of the investigations announced in November 1992 "into the incidents witnessed in Juba town in June and July 1992" which has apparently been submitted to the Council of Ministers. In addition, the government should establish independent and impartial investigations into reported extrajudicial executions and other human rights violations in the Nuba mountains; into extrajudicial executions and the abduction of women and children by PDF forces in northern Bahr al-Ghazal; and into all reports of torture and ill-treatment by military, security or other bodies working with the government.

SPLA-United should order investigations into abuses such as the deliberate and arbitrary killing of civilians by their forces in southern Upper Nile and Bahr al-Ghazal in 1991 and 1992; the killing of SPLA members thought to be loyal to the Mainstream faction in 1991; and the death of Nuba at Baliet in 1992.

SPLA-Mainstream should order investigations into abuses such as the deliberate and arbitrary killing of civilians in central Upper Nile in 1992 and 1993 and in Eastern Equatoria in 1992 and 1993; the torture of suspected opponents of the leadership arrested in the 1980s; the torture of detainees arrested since 1991; and the death of Martin Majier Gai and others in 1993.

Whenever human rights abuses are reported they should be investigated immediately.

Investigations must be seen to be thorough and impartial, and should always take place according to the following basic principles:

- the investigations should take place promptly;
- those conducting investigations should be empowered to obtain all the information necessary to the inquiry and to summon witnesses and officials allegedly involved in human rights violations to give evidence;
- action should be taken against any member of the military or security forces who refuses to cooperate with investigations;
- steps should be taken to safeguard complainants, witnesses and investigators in human rights cases against violence, threats of violence or any other form of intimidation;
- the investigative body should issue reports as soon as possible and these should immediately be made public. Reports should give details on the scope of investigations, should describe in detail what took place in the alleged incident, the evidence on which findings are based and the procedures used to evaluate evidence. In addition, they should make recommendations on effective, practical measures to prevent human rights violations or abuses. Those in authority should indicate the steps they intend to take in response;
- the authorities should be given a limited time within which they must respond to each report, indicating what action is being taken to remedy abuses and prevent their recurrence, and should make such responses public.

CHAPTER 8

4. Bring to justice all soldiers and officials responsible for human rights violations

There should be no impunity for the abuse of human rights. The **government** and the SPLAs should ensure that soldiers, security officials and others accused of involvement in human rights abuses are suspended from duty and removed from any positions in which they might be able to influence complainants, witnesses or others while the allegations against them are investigated. The **government** should ensure that soldiers, security officials and others against whom there is evidence of human rights violations should be brought to justice.

5. Take action to prevent extrajudicial executions and deliberate and arbitrary killings and to stop torture and ill-treatment

The **government** and both factions of the SPLA should ensure there is strict control, including a clear chain of command, over all military units and security or other officials responsible for the apprehension, arrest, detention, custody and imprisonment of prisoners:

- clear orders should be given prohibiting extrajudicial executions and deliberate and arbitrary killings;
- strict control should be exercised over all military units, PDF units, militia and security services engaged in operations in areas of armed conflict;
- records should be kept about anyone taken into detention, however brief this detention might be, by both the detaining military, security or police unit or authority, and any military, security or police unit or authority or prison receiving prisoners;
- written regulations governing procedures for the use of firearms should be issued to every soldier, PDF and other militia member and security official. In every incident where a firearm is discharged, a report should be made promptly to the competent authorities.

Government and senior SPLA officials should give a clear directive to soldiers, militia members and security officials that the violation of the basic human rights of civilians or detained combatants is not acceptable, whatever the circumstances, and will be punished:

- clear orders should be given prohibiting all forms of torture and

125

ill-treatment, including rape, beatings, and, in all cases, the killing of prisoners;

- all members of the military, security services or any militia should have the established right and duty to disobey any such orders that are given.

The **government** and both factions of the SPLA should produce guidelines to safeguard the human rights of detainees under interrogation:

- clear records should be kept, including the date, time and duration, of each period of interrogation, as well as the names of all those present;
- these records should be open to judicial scrutiny and to inspection by lawyers and relatives of detainees;
- when prisoners complain that confessions have been extracted under torture, the burden should be on the detaining and interrogating authorities to prove that the confession was voluntary and that torture and ill-treatment did not occur.

The **government** should ratify the UN Convention against Torture and Other Cruel, Inhuman or Degrading Treatment or Punishment.

The **government** and each faction of the SPLA should allow immediate access by qualified, independent inspectors from internationally recognized humanitarian organizations to all places of custody, including security service offices, on a regular basis. The inspectors should be allowed to make unannounced visits and have unrestricted access to all prisoners. The **government** and each faction of the SPLA should publicly commit themselves to abide by the humanitarian principles enshrined in the Geneva Conventions of 1949.

6. End arbitrary detention

Both the government and each faction of the SPLA should immediately and unconditionally release any prisoner detained solely for the non-violent expression of conscientiously held beliefs or because of his or her ethnic origin. The government should remove the legal and constitutional provisions allowing administrative detention without charge or trial. All prisoners should be promptly produced in court and charged with a recognizably criminal offence, otherwise they should be released.

Until administrative detention is discontinued, the **government**

CHAPTER 8

should introduce effective safeguards to protect the rights of detainees. In particular:

- prisoners should not be kept in detention after their release has been ordered and should not be redetained on the basis of new detention orders, unless the latter contain previously unavailable, clear reasons for arrest of which the authorities were unaware at the time of initial release;

- the expression of non-violent political views, the staging of work-stoppages and the holding of non-violent political meetings should be excluded from the scope of the legal and constitutional provisions allowing administrative detention.

In both **government** areas and SPLA-held zones, everyone should be informed, at the time of their arrest, of the specific reasons for their arrest:

- all detainees should have access to relatives, independent medical personnel and lawyers promptly after arrest and regularly throughout their period in custody;

- relatives should be informed immediately of any arrest and should be kept informed of the detainee's whereabouts at all times;

- the **government** and the SPLAs should keep central registries to receive information about the names and whereabouts of all persons detained without charge.

7. Ensure fair trials

In any judicial proceeding, any confession or evidence established to have been obtained as a result of torture should not be accepted as evidence. Judges should be required to exclude all such evidence (except when it is being used as evidence against a person accused of torture that a statement was obtained under torture).

The **government** should end the use of courts-martial, whose procedures fall far short of international standards of fair trial. They should be replaced by courts which contain procedural safeguards protecting basic human rights.

The **government** should review procedures in Public Order Courts to ensure that defendants have adequate time and facilities to prepare a defence, access to defence counsel of their own choosing, and the right of automatic appeal to a higher court.

'THE TEARS OF ORPHANS'

8. Compensate the victims

The **government** should provide fair compensation to the victims of all human rights violations or, in the case of those killed or "disappeared", to their immediate relatives.

9. The government should end the ill-treatment of street children

The **government** should issue strict instructions prohibiting torture and ill-treatment, to police and any other body, official or non-governmental, involved in the rounding-up of street children.

- The use of leg-irons, flogging and any other forms of cruel, inhuman or degrading punishment or treatment in special camps or schools should be immediately banned.

- A central registry of children taken into special camps or schools should be established to facilitate searches by families for their children. Information provided by children about the identity of their relatives should be acted on so that they can be reunited.

10. The government should take immediate steps to reunite with their families women and children abducted from northern Bahr al-Ghazal and the Nuba mountains

Strict instructions should be issued to all soldiers, PDF and other militia members, forbidding abduction. The authorities should investigate all reported abductions and instances of alleged slave-holding with a view to releasing victims and bringing criminal proceedings against those responsible for the initial abduction and subsequent trafficking. The authorities should provide families searching for their missing relatives with the fullest official cooperation.

11. The government should abolish cruel, inhuman or degrading punishments in law

The punishments of stoning to death, crucifixion, mutilation and flogging should be removed from the Penal Code 1991. Pending their abolition, the sentences of flogging and mutilation should be suspended. All amputation and death sentences should be commuted. The death penalty should be abolished.

II. Recommendations to the international community

The international community should ensure that the Sudan

CHAPTER 8

Government and both factions of the SPLA respect internationally recognized human rights and humanitarian standards by:

- promoting and supporting the deployment of an international civilian human rights monitoring body mandated to monitor the situation of human rights in all parts of the country;
- ensuring that human rights issues are addressed as a central part of any peace agreement;
- providing the UN Special Rapporteur on Sudan with all the support necessary for him to discharge his mandate thoroughly and effectively;
- seeking additional ways to support those in Sudan working to defend human rights.

'THE TEARS OF ORPHANS'

ENDNOTES

[1] *Sudan: A continuing human rights crisis* (AI Index: AFR 54/03/92).

[2] The 17 *in absentia*, who included senior political opponents of the government, were all in exile.

[3] *Comments by the Government of Sudan on the report of the Special Rapporteur*, 18 February 1994, page 31

[4] UN Doc. E/CN.44/1986/15, at. 48

[5] UN Doc. E/CN.4/1994/48, at. 59-61

[6] Rape inside marriage is punishable by up to 100 lashes.

[7] *Quantifying genocide in the southern Sudan 1983-1993* by Millard Burr, issued by the US Committee for Refugees

[8] *United Nations 1994 consolidated inter-agency appeal: Sudan*, issued by the Department of Humanitarian Affairs

[9] Amnesty International has previously reported that at least 230 people were arrested in Juba (*Sudan: The ravages of war: political killings and humanitarian disaster*, AI Index: AFR 54/29/93, September 1993). In March 1994 the organization learned the names of 70 prisoners reported to be held in northern Sudan. Few were previously known to the organization.

[10] UN Doc. CRC/C/3/Add. 20

[11] Amnesty International uses the phrase "deliberate and arbitrary killing" to denote wilful and unlawful killings committed on the authority of an armed political group or with its acquiescence. Like the Sudan Government, the SPLA is bound by the principles of international humanitarian law which protects the rights of civilians and others not taking part in the hostilities during armed conflict.

[12] These events are described in greater detail in a report by Human Rights Watch/Africa, Civilian devastation: abuses by all parties in the war in southern Sudan, 1994.

[13] UN Doc. E/CN.4/1994/7, para. 566

[14] UN Doc. E/CN.4/1994/48

[15] *Ibid.*

[16] *Ibid.*

APPENDIX

SUDAN'S OBLIGATIONS UNDER INTERNATIONAL LAW (As of October 1994)

Sudan has ratified or acceded to various international human rights treaties. Although many were signed by previous governments, the current government remains obligated to respect their provisions. Sudan is party to the following UN treaties:

- the International Covenant on Civil and Political Rights, acceded to on 18 March 1986. However, Sudan has not become a party to either the First or Second Optional Protocols;
- the International Covenant on Economic, Social and Cultural Rights, *acceded to on 18 March 1986;*
- the International Convention on the Elimination of all Forms of Racial Discrimination, acceded to on 21 March 1977;
- the Slavery Convention, as amended, succeeded to on 9 September *1957;*
- the Supplementary Convention on the Abolition of Slavery, the Slave Trade, and Institutions and Practices Similar to Slavery, succeeded to on 9 September 1957;
- the Convention relating to the Status of Refugees, acceded to on 22 *February 1974, and its Additional Protocol relating to the Status of Refugees, acceded to on 23 May 1974;*
- the Convention on the Rights of the Child, ratified on 3 August 1990.

On 4 June 1986 Sudan signed the Convention against Torture and Other Cruel, Inhuman or Degrading Treatment or Punishment. Although it has yet to ratify the Convention, Sudan is obligated under international law not to take any action which would defeat its objective and purpose.

As a member of the ILO, Sudan has ratified the following Conventions:

- Convention (No. 29) concerning Forced or Compulsory Labour;
- Convention (No. 98) concerning the Application of the Principles of the Right to Organise and Bargain Collectively, ratified on 18 June 1957;
- Convention (No. 105) concerning the Abolition of Forced Labour, *ratified on 22 October 1970;*
- Convention (No. 111) concerning Discrimination in Respect of Employment and Occupation, *ratified on 22 October 1970;*
- Convention (No. 122) concerning Employment Policy.

On 23 September 1957 Sudan acceded to the four Geneva Conventions of 1949. Common Article 3 applies to all parties involved in internal armed conflicts — armed opposition groups as well as governments. As of 30 June 1993, Sudan had not ratified either of the two Additional Protocols to the Geneva Conventions.

APPENDIX

As a member of the Organization of African Unity (OAU), Sudan has ratified:
- the African Charter on Human and Peoples' Rights, ratified on 11 March 1986;
- the OAU Convention governing the Specific Aspects of Refugee Problems in Africa, ratified on 12 January 1975.